OUT OF SIBERIA: LIESEL'S EXILE

CHARLOTTE HOFMANN-HEGE

ISBN: 978-1-212270-38-5

1st & 2nd English editions 2016; 3rd edition 2017; 4th edition 2019

Printers:
For The Right Reasons
38-40 Grant Street
Inverness
IV3 8BN
fortherightreasons@rocketmail.com

Typesetting & design:
DUFI Art
www.dufi-art.com

*This translation is dedicated
to the memory of Elizabeth.*

CONTENTS

'There is a saying – Truth is stranger than fiction - and this is certainly true of this amazing story. It tells of the life of one woman, spanning the 20th century and everything that devastated Europe during that time. It is a story of exile and heartbreak, but also of fortitude and hope. Such a story has a special appeal now in the 21st century, when so many others are experiencing separation from their native countries and communities. Liesel's adventures cannot but create a deeper appreciation of the suffering of displaced people throughout the world. I commend this translation as a faithful and excellent replication of the original.'

Angus Ross, former senior examiner in German, SQA

'This book is so moving, so poignant and relevant to today's issues. Not only do we see man's inhumanity to man, but more importantly Liesel's narrative highlights the victory of love, faith and goodness over the horrors of the Nazi, Stalin era. I strongly feel that it should become prescribed reading for every secondary pupil in this country.'

Fay Henderson, retired lecturer

'This is a most intriguing and moving story. I have been left with profound admiration for Liesel and her ability to withstand such appalling treatment. The author's straightforward style brings us into the heart of each situation Liesel faces. The impact is arresting. Would that a story as rare as this one featured in the syllabus of our schools and colleges.'

John Henderson, retired lecturer

'I am just writing to say how much I enjoyed & appreciated 'Out of Siberia:Liesel's Exile'. What a story...it is very moving & heart-rending. What an eye-opener into life under Stalin. Congratulations on the excellent quality of the production & presentation.'

Lionel Holmes

'I have just finished reading 'Out of Siberia: Liesel's Exile'. I enjoyed it so much. What a remarkable story of suffering, endurance, faith in God and finally freedom. Without her faith in God, Liesel's life would have been so depressing and tragic.'

Vivian Ferido, California

OUT OF SIBERIA: LIESEL'S EXILE

Painting by Vladimir Zhdanov

Cheerfully confident and full of enthusiasm, Liesel set out in 1912 as a young German girl to stay with her uncle and aunt in the Ukraine.

"This is a wonderful land", she wrote in her first letter home. Little did she realize that she would spend more than 30 years exiled in Siberia. There she became an outcast, a refugee and a widow, losing not only her husband but all five of her children. Moreover, she subsequently faced a traumatic readjustment among her family and community when she eventually returned to Germany after 55 years.

Such an extraordinary life has found an ideal biographer. Her cousin, Charlotte Hofmann-Hege, has drawn on Liesel's correspondence with great skill and sensitivity. The result is a captivating account of someone's triumph over tragedy. Few would disagree with her suggestion that Liesel "represents millions of people today who are forcibly deprived of their rights."

But what sustained Liesel under such prolonged pressure? God's promise: "I will never leave you or forsake you."

1

FIRST ENCOUNTER

Gardens - Heilbronn

Yesterday I made one of my regular visits to the public gardens in Heilbronn. They looked beautiful. It was there that, quite by chance, I met Elizabeth Thiessen for the first time as she was sitting on one of the park seats. I had no idea that this rather strange looking lady was a cousin of mine.

At that time our children still attended school in Heilbronn and, on the afternoon of this particular day, I was waiting for them at our rendezvous - the very seat where I met Elizabeth - so that we might travel home together.

A glance at the woman next to me revealed someone who was soberly dressed and well advanced in years. Her appearance reminded me of a certain kind of female settler who had returned from the east, and in fact I took her to be just such a person when I saw her that afternoon.

She had a pale complexion, and the slight squint in her right eye gave her face in repose the look of someone who was lost in thought. I passed one or two trivial remarks to which she responded in a slightly foreign accent.

Just at that moment my children rushed up to where we were sitting. Rosy-cheeked and bright-eyed, they were bursting to share news of all the latest excitement that had made their day. I bade farewell to the stranger on the seat and we made our way to the car.

My parting words required only a second to utter, yet how I later regretted that brief instant. I was scarcely aware of the fact that my friendliness towards this stranger was tinged with pity, and a not a very wholesome sympathy either. I was sorry for a thoroughly patronizing attitude. At heart I was rather pleased that my lot was not that of any asylum-seeker or a returning patriot. I was not forced, as they are, to seek some small corner in our over-populated and environmentally insecure Federal Republic of Germany.

What did I really know about the terrible pressures that can afflict a person today in the treadmill of existence?

Several months later I met Elizabeth again. My brother had invited us to his house with the intention of getting us acquainted with each other. In the meantime I had learned that this unknown cousin of mine had settled in Heilbronn, and that she had a most unusual story. Nevertheless, it took me quite a while before I recognized her as the woman I had encountered that afternoon in the public gardens. For one thing, she was dressed in a distinctively western style, and she appeared younger and more cheerful. Incidentally, she did not remember me for which I was glad, and I held my peace.

She spoke of her experiences in a lively manner, almost in a jocular, humorous vein that often lacked any logical sequence. In addition, she still manifested difficulty in expressing herself in German. Everyone knew her as "Liesel", the name that she had become used to since childhood.

After this meeting Liesel lived for about another 12 years in and around Heilbronn. We often used to see one another and exchange news. On many occasions she spoke about her past experiences, although the information I gleaned was not always what I was looking for. To be sure, Liesel was a trifle unconventional. When she died in 1982 the family asked me to write an account of her extraordinary life. I received a case of tattered letters, yellowed with age, several tape recordings and notebooks in which were what looked like diary entries.

There is no point in pretending that I found the task of compiling this biography other than arduous. To be honest, I did not find Liesel an easy person to get on with, and it was plain that there were two sides to her character. I struggled with the interpretation of her artless jottings. Were they really substantial enough to form the basis of a biography?

However, the more I delved into Liesel's story, the greater the impact it made on me. This was because, although in the first instance I was investigating the life of an individual, it struck me that her case was representative of millions of people who have been forcibly deprived of their rights in a world that is being regimented so heartlessly. There can be little doubt that, as long as humanity continues to multiply so precociously over the face of the earth, the forces of lust for power, money, violence, injustice and corruption, along with the misery arising from these evils, will not diminish. Kings and statesmen can easily command a hearing; but the marginalized people of society suffer silently and privately. Like a ghostly apparition, poverty assumes ever newer guises as it stealthily invades the nations. In each century it bears a characteristic feature, yet at the individual level it brings an inexorable challenge to face its bitter consequences.

Elizabeth's story is about one individual, and it is intended to give a voice to the voiceless. Thus it may be that what apparently belongs to the past speaks directly to our present situation. There are certainly many more personal histories of this sort than we realize.

During the course of my work I found myself compelled to change my mind on several occasions. I came to acknowledge the fact that in assessing someone's life, the issue is ultimately not merely about the maturity of their character or the irrefutable "greatness" of a particular achievement. Success in each enterprise involves looking beyond such factors, so that the eventual picture draws on very different, and more comprehensive criteria. When a biography is tackled from that standpoint it will not be difficult for the reader to discern these characteristics in Elizabeth Thiessen's life.

There is no doubt in my mind that, in the midst of so much spiritual searching, Elizabeth's biography offers encouragement, comfort and hope to those who are distracted and confused in today's world.

THE FAMILY HOME

Deutschhof - Heilbronn (1908)

"Every newly born child proclaims the message that God's trust in mankind is not yet exhausted."

Rabindranath Tagore

It seemed as if that summer of 1897 was darkened by a host of sorrows. In the kingdom of Württemberg a particularly severe hailstorm had destroyed half of the harvest, whilst in the kingdom of Bavaria the fields were drowned by flash floods after weeks of dry weather. The town of Schweinfurt am Main was on the point of being flooded more than once, and maize in the surrounding fields of the Deutschhof had to be ploughed up. Consequently, the happy Friday that dawned on the Deutschhof in July was especially welcome. "We have been blessed!" exclaimed the midwife excitedly as she patted the raucous infant on its rosy behind. "It's a girl! And I feel she is going to be plucky and strong. What a lovely shock of black hair she has on her little head. I'll soon be finished with the baby."

Whilst the midwife bathed the infant and wrapped her up she turned to the mother and asked her eagerly. "What name do you hope to give the little one? Of course it must have a name even if you Mennonites don't believe in baptism and let your youngsters grow up like heathens! But it's fine, isn't it, that with a girl you don't need to concern yourself with campaigning for exemption from home guard duty."

She did not venture to say any more, but it sometimes appeared to her as if the little community of Mennonites was somewhat stubborn. Yet for all that the Mennonites were really good people who often had large families. She certainly did not want to spoil her relationship with them.

"We want to call our little girl Elizabeth," the young mother replied warmly. But then she sighed: "Oh, sometimes I am afraid that I have inherited from my mother the tendency to have many children. She had to bring up a dozen boys and girls."

"Now that wouldn't be so bad," the midwife interjected, "if they were all the same kind of capable people that mother and grandmother are, would it?"

"Well, I'm not just as robust as them, so I couldn't undertake all that they did," mother Anna replied quietly.

At that point the midwife took her notebook and pencil, and with calm deliberation she made a new entry: 'Elizabeth Muselmann, 3rd child of farmer David Muselmann and his wife Anna (nee Hege). At Deutschhof near Scweinfurt, 20th July 1897.'

Only then did she allow the father to come into the maternity room. Such was the way of things in time past.

David Muselmann carried his two little children to see their newborn sister. In one arm he carried two year old Christian, a delicate youngster, and in the other arm he held Heinrich, a plump and sturdy one year old.

"Well, Anna, mother and child were nearly going to celebrate the same birthday!" he called out cheerily. "It will be yours in 3 days' time", he said as he bent down to kiss his wife gently on the forehead as an expression of his gratitude. He was delighted at the safe arrival of a healthy daughter.

"Summer's child! She will surely grow up healthy and strong!"

Anna smiled warmly, but then she grew pensive. She remembered how her father had often told her that the day on which she herself had been born must have been a particularly difficult one in many ways. For one thing, the war of 1870 had flared up so quickly that both her parents were overcome by despair. Their apprehension arose from the consequences of their pacifist convictions as Mennonites. The fact was that this group had for centuries desisted from any sort of armed conflict on the basis of the command: "You shall not kill". Of course it was impossible to foresee on that day that the conflict would end favourably for Germany.

As the eldest of the children Anna, gifted Anna, had to support her mother from early on in her life. There was scarcely ever time for lessons and reading books, far less for carefree child's play. And now she was 27 years old, and had to manage a large farm along with caring for her husband David. In addition, as from today, she had 3 little children, and she felt exhausted into the bargain. However, it would not do for anyone to notice her tiredness. Above all, the last thing she wanted was for her husband to be upset in any way. He looked severely strained, for the precarious state of agriculture in Germany at the close of the 19th century caused him many a headache.

That evening David Muselmann told Anna's parents the good news about the birth of their grand-daughter. Anna's parents managed Breitenau farm situated in the lowlands of Baden-Württemberg. Thereafter he plucked a couple of roses from the garden in order to brighten up the living-room. Before he himself went to bed he said the customary evening prayer over his little daughter's cradle as she slipped peacefully into her first night's sleep on earth.

In fact it began to look as if Anna's presentiments about being a prolific child-bearer, as her mother was, were being fulfilled. After Liesel, as she was now commonly known, there arrived in quick succession another two sisters and two brothers.

However, when the seventh, little Rudi, arrived, Anna knew that this would be her last child. Her husband's state of health had changed dramatically for the worse. Anna had enough experience to know that it would be fatal to take any risks with tuberculosis, an illness which at that time was so great a scourge of humanity. Although Robert Koch had identified the tubercle bacillus twenty years previously, there was still complete ignorance as to how consumption should be dealt with if someone had already lost a good deal of their resistance. Indeed, some people were already treating David as if he was a leper. Anna drew on all the reserves of her will-power to fight off nagging fears and weakness. Yet there was many a day when she was overcome by the sombre foreboding that, in the long run, even she would not get the better of this pernicious illness.

At all events the children must be spared the effects of consumption. Both parents exerted themselves strenuously to this end and, with the exception of the eldest child, who was rather frail, they all grew up healthy. They were ignorant of what it had cost their parents to ensure this good start. The farm steading itself was well appointed, enjoying open access to the surrounding countryside, and this was an ideal environment for youngsters to grow up in. The brother and sister, Heinrich and Liesel were sometimes rather boisterous and prone to outbursts of temper. However, they were both also clearly of a conciliatory nature, as well as being helpful and good-natured. Admittedly there were occasions when Anna could have wished that her eldest daughter acted in a more demure and responsible way. Not long after she had started school her teacher described her as a bit of a tomboy. Anna could never have guessed that a time would come when exactly this robust disposition would stand her daughter in good stead.

When Liesel was just in her first year at school there was a wonderful family Christmas gathering that made an indelible impression on her mind. As the sitting room doors burst open to reveal all that had been prepared for that Christmas day, the little girl imagined that she might in fact be shown the glory of heaven. Little Rudi, who was one year old, uttered a cry of delight when his sisters led him up to the Christmas tree. Whilst Anna played the piano the children sang the carol: "The lights are shining on the Christmas tree". Liesel's Christmas present to her parents was to write out this carol in large letters, just as a child would copy them.

The second verse is as follows:

"Two angels entered silently,
Concealed from human sight,
They prayed beside the Christmas tree
Then turned and took their flight."

The child looked across to her father who was sitting in the corner of the room coughing. Suddenly it seemed as if he was surrounded by light - could it be the angels who had come to greet him? Were they perhaps the very angels who were ready to take him into eternity? Liesel was often sensitive to things that other people missed. She quickly turned aside and began to sob.

"Cry baby!" mocked her brothers. "And at Christmas of all times, just when everything was so lovely!"

Years later in old age, Liesel was to write with a shaky hand these words underneath the same verses which she had copied out as a child and which she had kept: "This was to be our last Christmas festival together with our beloved father. I sensed it; I knew it; and I began to cry bitterly."

All of a sudden that dreaded day came. · It was a bright, clear morning in the early spring of 1905. Grandpa Christian Hege and Grandma Lenchen had travelled specially from Breitenau in order to support their daughter. The older children had been sent to stay with other relatives. Liesel was continually squabbling with Heinrich about a red rubber ball which their father had brought back from a recent trip to Würzburg. Although they were both very fond of each other, it was exactly on that account that Liesel and Heinrich would regularly fall out with each other.

"You always insist that the ball is yours alone!" shouted Heinrich angrily as he grabbed his eight year old sister roughly by her lustrous black plaits. "Now it's my turn to have it!"

"Now children, how can you possibly argue with one another at this time?" pleaded Grandpa Christian, who had just come in the front door. Whenever he spoke with his grandchildren his voice was always mellow and kindly. However, today both children detected such a note of sorrow in his speech that they retreated into a stunned silence.

To be sure, Grandpa was feeling really low. Laid out in the bedroom his son-in-law, who had just turned 37, was fast approaching death. The fever had taken its toll. What pain it caused him to think that his eldest daughter Anna, so nimble and active, should be afflicted with such a fate. In those days the lot of widows was hard indeed.

Christian was a godly man, but present circumstances placed his faith under severe strain. Even the resilient Anna was not as healthy as usual. He had noticed beforehand the red patches on her cheeks that signified fever; and it was on account of this illness that he had already buried his oldest son. The grief at losing so gifted a young life suddenly overwhelmed him once again.

Little Rudi, who had just celebrated his second birthday, slid in between his grandfather's feet. He wanted to be near the old man. Grandpa Christian had a happy knack of winning over young children, and he was somehow comforted by Rudi's little hand.

"Try playing something quieter, children", he suggested to Heinrich and Liesel.

"That's fine," exclaimed Liesel, "so let's play hide and seek." She promptly disappeared behind the bushes in the garden. With amazing agility he glided between the trees, and then clambered onto the fork of a bough. That was the base which she defended with spirit against the attacks of her brothers. She clung tightly to the rubber ball. For Liesel it represented something tangible of her father. No human being could tell how sad she felt today. Of all the children she was the one who depended most upon her dear father. And exactly because of that she would today be especially rebellious and wild. Dear Liesel, what is it that you want to hide from? The pain? Fate? One day it will overtake you.

Someone called to her from the house, but she did not move. Liesel sensed the deathly silence that had descended over the farm-yard. That which she most feared had happened. Father was dead.

Anna immediately addressed herself as mother to the extra responsibilities which had befallen her with courage and resourcefulness, but her strength was limited.

"Kiev is usually known as the mother of all Russian cities", explained her uncle. "It was in this place that the Orthodox Christian faith began through the influence of Prince Vladimir in 988. Christians used to be baptized in the Dnieper." Liesel spent an entrancing time viewing the legendary cathedral of St. Sophia. She was mesmerized by the brilliant ceramic icons which covered the walls of the cathedral. As she walked round the sanctuary her eyes took in new wonders at every turn: frescos, mosaics and a host of marble and alabaster columns. "It may be that this is your one and only chance to see such a wonderful church," whispered aunt Frida. "By contrast our Mennonite churches are certainly uninspiring."

On and on they travelled into the vast hinterland of Russia. Forests, plains and meadows seemed to beckon to them through the carriage windows as they stretched away into the far distance.

At long last they arrived at Charkov. Right behind the town were the quarters in which the German population had settled. Their dwellings were easily identifiable by their decorated houses and neat terraced gardens. The terminus of their journey lay on the river Molotschna, a small river which ran into Lake Asowsche. It was here that the Mennonite community had gathered, having built the two towns Halbstadt and Gnadenfeld. Both towns covered an area approximately equal to that lying between Heidelberg and Stuttgart.

Having to make do on her first night with rather makeshift accomodation, Liesel spent much of the long night awake. It was the strangeness of her new surroundings as well as the new smells which aroused in her mild anxiety. It was a good thing that she slept in the same room as some of the children, otherwise she might easily have been overcome with homesickness.

Aunt Frida looked in briefly to see how she was. "Are you still awake, my child?" she enquired kindly. "Of course there are so many things that are completely new to you; but don't worry. Everything will soon fall into place."

As she eventually closed her eyes, Liesel's mind was still full of the many scenes that she had encountered on their journey: the rivers, the cities and the never ending forests and meadows. The sheer scale of all that she had seen overwhelmed her, so that she seemed to herself to be

Misprints

page 13 and 21 are same page.

"Mother was such a good and upright person," Liesel would often say of her. There is little doubt that the young woman prepared her children for the battles of life with great honesty and conviction. As the moonlight shone into the children's bedroom, she would sit by their little beds and repeat their prayers with them as if she was appealing directly to God.

The picture which Liesel retained of her mother was of her dark, slim figure silhouetted against the bright moonlight, although she was not a religious child. In fact she was frequently erratic and disobedient, and the only thing in which she showed any kind of persistence was piano playing.

Nonetheless, the memory of her childhood shone brightly within her like a guiding star, and nothing in her future experience could ever completely eradicate that happy phase of her life.

Fortunately Grandpa Christian was spared the information about Anna's terminal illness as he died quite suddenly of pneumonia two years after his son-in-law David.

The last weeks of Anna's life were particularly hard. For the sake of her beloved children she withstood the claims of death valiantly for as long as she could. Even during feverish turns, when her mind was sometimes clouded, she devoted herself entirely to the welfare of her children. One evening when she appeared to be disturbed, she cried out as though she had seen a vision, "Do not let Liesel travel abroad!" Then on a mild day in March 1908 her fight was over, and the 38 year old widow was laid to rest next to her husband in the graveyard at Schweinfurt. She left behind seven children aged between five and thirteen years.

The Court of Chancery at Schweinfurt appointed a master baker as guardian over the children, but it was clear that he was not capable of fulfilling his responsibilities, and he had no idea how to maintain the estate. It was no longer possible for the oldest son to keep the farm.

Now what was to happen to the seven children? During the brief spell in which they were alone they had grown together. It was not permitted to separate them or to send them to different families. It was at this point that Grandma Lenchen decided to take all the seven grandchildren and bring them up at Breitenau in her own home. (Today Breitenau is well-known on account of the lake there which is a popular tourist attraction.) She was by now a widow herself, and she had already borne 19 children of her own, of whom she had buried two sons and three daughters. Anna's brother Hans undertook the task of father in place of David who had died so unexpectedly.

For Liesel the train journey from Schweinfurt to Heilbronn via Würzburg remained an unforgettable experience. Marienburg castle overlooking the river Main seemed like a fairy-castle from a story book. Because children are not normally given to reflection, Liesel's curiosity concerning the future was a stronger impulse in her than the inclination to be homesick for the past. That tendency did not awaken in her until much later.

The lowland areas of Württemberg are charming: vineyards and splendid fruit-trees greeted the children on their arrival in Breitenau. The youthful Uncle Hans Hege, Anna's brother, was still single, and his younger brothers were either training or studying. The generations were so close together that the youngest uncle was only five years older than Liesel. She was particularly fond of Uncle Fritz who was a strikingly handsome blond youth seven years older than Liesel. However, it seemed that Fritz was unaware of Liesel's affections.

As Anna had brought up all her children to be independent, they soon settled in well to the comfortable home of their grandmother which was so full of interest and vitality. Breitenau farm was surrounded by the Lowenstern hills. This lovely setting, high above the surrounding countryside, became their new home.

"DO NOT LET LIESEL TRAVEL ABROAD!"

Breitenau

"It is not those who are fulfilled, but those who are not fulfilled who need our love."

Oscar Wilde.

"The most important thing for Liesel is that she learns to sew well." That was Grandma's decision after her granddaughter had finished her schooling. "Who knows, she may be able to make a career for herself as a dress-maker." Clothes off the peg were unknown then.

As a result Liesel was sent to a good school for seamstresses in Heilbronn. A photo taken at that time shows her as a pretty girl in the midst of her fellow pupils. There is a suggestion of audacity behind the bright smile. "Such was her nature," confided one of her former classmates. "To begin with she pulled our plaits and hair-curlers, which were then all the rage. She wanted to test if everything was genuine, for not everyone had hair that was as beautiful as Elizabeth's."

Even Grandma had trouble controlling her lively grand-daughter.

The household chores were in no way eased for the elderly lady, particularly as her own daughters had meantime got married and had left home. It was only later that she discovered how conscientious her own daughters had been when she saw how Liesel preferred playing around with the young grandchildren in the garden to working in the sewing room where help was so much needed.

"She needs the control of younger and stronger hands," Grandma would occasionally say. "Then it might be possible to make something of her."

Every summer Breitenau was the scene of much colourful activity. Most of Anna's sisters took it in turn to visit the farmstead with their children. Then there was the annual influx of Mennonite students from the missionary college in Basel. Most of these young people came from Canada and the Ukraine, but there were also representatives of other nations too. They were always given their keep when they came to help with the harvest during the holidays.

One of those who came during the summer holidays was a lively student called Benjamin Unruh. It was he who courted and won the hand of Anna's sister, Frida, an intelligent and beautiful girl. They later returned to Benjamin's homeland in the Ukraine where he became a lecturer in theology in the city of Halbstadt bei Charkow.

In 1911 the young family spent an extended holiday visiting at Breitenau. Aunt Frida was expecting their fourth child which was due to be born in November of that year. Liesel felt particularly drawn to this quiet, upright young woman who reminded her so much of her deceased mother. But who was the one to raise the possibility of Liesel accompanying Frida on her return to Russia after the birth of little Heini? Might it not well have been the Grandmother, who by now found it next to impossible to cope with the 15 year old?

Certainly Aunt Frida urgently needed someone to help her at home having had four children in the space of four years. For his part uncle Benjamin was favourably disposed to the idea that this might be a way for his wife to recieve help. Liesel was ideally suited to the task as she was physically robust and could handle a lot of work. However, uncle Hans was politically astute and he was the only one to voice reservations.

17

"I am not all sure," he commented, "that life in Russia is as peaceful as you describe it, Benjamin. After all," he continued, "the country is in the grip of revolutionaries, and you know that countless people lost their lives a year or so ago (1905) in the "Bloody Sunday" massacre. Also many Russians have emigrated from there and have settled in Württemberg. Then the Czar is weak ... Russia lost the war with Japan ... and there is continual unrest in the Crimea which is, after all, not so far away from you."

Uncle Benjamin smiled good-naturedly. "Hans," he replied, "you cannot really compare Russia with the German Empire. It is the largest country in the world which occupies a significant area of the earth's surface. It is peopled by many colourful races who speak a whole variety of languages. If some crisis erupts in the north news of it is not heard in the south of the country until a good while later. All the same, our Czar chose a German princess as his wife. Moreover, the two daughters of the Czar, Katherine and Olga, who were both queens in Württemberg, have earned your love and respect. Should the present Czar prove to be a weak ruler, he has nonetheless been chosen by us Mennonites. Freedom of worship and release from military service have been guaranteed for us by statute. We have a proverb which says, "If the heavens are high, the Czar's powers on earth are as broad." Russia! Goodness, what can you dear people know about Russia here in Germany, where you are surrounded and hemmed in by so many other nations?"

Whenever he thought about his homeland Uncle Benjamin used to become quite emotional. "Why", he exclaimed, "you can scarcely imagine what our magnificent farmsteads are like, nor the vast wheat fields that stretch away to the horizon like an ocean! Above them is the canopy of the deep blue sky. What a wonderful sight! Liesel will certainly love being with us."

For a moment the others in the room were silent. Could it be that they had become aware of mother Anna's final entreaty: "Don't let Liesel go abroad!"?

Uncle Benjamin continued, as though he had been conscious of this unspoken appeal: "Do not worry; there is no need to view the Ukraine as some sort of isolated place. After all there are already so many Germans living there. In addition, I cannot foresee Liesel spending more than 18 months to 2 years with us. By that time we should be over the worst as far as the needs of the children are concerned. Meantime she can begin to learn Russian as well as further her education in a German school, if she wants. The different circumstances there will certainly broaden her horizon." The details of the journey were explained to Liesel.

"I am really quite happy to get away from Breitenau," thought Liesel to herself with easy nonchalance. "Of course it is beautiful here, and life is pretty good; but now everyone is trying to get at me. Frankly, I just don't fit in to this very religious household as I once used to. No; I'm not about to dance to everybody else's tune! Now that I'm fifteen years old I am no longer a child. Uncle Benjamin is certainly not strict with me, and I've already taken sweet Aunt Frida to my heart. Of course, I have to acknowledge that there would be a lot of work with the little children; but then there is nowhere on the face of this earth in which you can get away with not working. I learned that long ago!"

Is it the outward circumstances or specific talents which determine a person's destiny? Supposing that Liesel had been more amenable to her grandmother and had become indispensable to her, it is almost certain that she would never have released her, even for the sake of helping Frida. Or are we swept up in much greater circumstances? Is everything ordered and pre-planned beforehand, as mother Anna's fearful cry suggested?

It was in the spring of 1912 that the Unruh family set out with their four young children and Liesel for the Ukraine. Taking leave of the family was no easy matter. Even Aunt Frida was touched by the occasion, in spite of the fact that, true to her nature, she showed little feeling outwardly. Liesel herself, as she hugged her brothers and sisters farewell, was visibly moved by the significance of this leave-taking. They all travelled together in the coach to the station. One final kiss and wave, and then Breitenau vanished from view. Uncle Hans' fiancée, Aunt Julie, tarried on the platform of Willsbach station as she had brought a special farewell gift. For her part, Liesel hung out of the carriage window long after the train had pulled out of the station, until at last there was nothing more to see of their beloved faces.

Usually it is easier for those who are departing than for those who remain to get over the pain of separation. All the new impressions which they encounter soon help to eradicate their sorrows. Even so in Liesel's case, her attention was soon absorbed by the many fresh and exciting experiences which took up her attention.

"IT IS A WONDERFUL COUNTRY"

Kiev and Dnieper River

"It is pointless trying to understand Russia with one's mind, or by any other normal standards. One can only comprehend Russia with the heart."

Fyodor Tjuttschew, 19th century.

This kingdom of the Czars - what an incredible land Russia is! Liesel had already heard of the giants, such formidable characters as Tolstoy and Tchaikovsky. Initially she had imagined to herself a rather plain, even formidable landscape. Now as she was travelling through it, she was delighted with the bright, seemingly endless horizons that opened up before her. At each stop along the way she scrutinized with intense interest the names on the station platforms.

Then they transversed the Dneiper. What a magnificent river it was! To Liesel it seemed as wide as the sea itself. Immediately her mind flew back to the rivers she had grown up to know at home, the Main and Neckar. Another unforgettable impression was their entry into Kiev on the railway. How the many golden turrets and towers in the city gleamed in the evening sunshine.

"Kiev is usually known as the mother of all Russian cities", explained her uncle. "It was in this place that the Orthodox Christian faith began through the influence of Prince Vladimir in 988. Christians used to be baptized in the Dnieper." Liesel spent an entrancing time viewing the legendary cathedral of St. Sophia. She was mesmerized by the brilliant ceramic icons which covered the walls of the cathedral. As she walked round the sanctuary her eyes took in new wonders at every turn: frescos, mosaics and a host of marble and alabaster columns. "It may be that this is your one and only chance to see such a wonderful church," whispered aunt Frida. "By contrast our Mennonite churches are certainly uninspiring."

On and on they travelled into the vast hinterland of Russia. Forests, plains and meadows seemed to beckon to them through the carriage windows as they stretched away into the far distance.

At long last they arrived at Charkov. Right behind the town were the quarters in which the German population had settled. Their dwellings were easily identifiable by their decorated houses and neat terraced gardens. The terminus of their journey lay on the river Molotschna, a small river which ran into Lake Asowsche. It was here that the Mennonite community had gathered, having built the two towns Halbstadt and Gnadenfeld. Both towns covered an area approximately equal to that lying between Heidelberg and Stuttgart.

Having to make do on her first night with rather makeshift accomodation, Liesel spent much of the long night awake. It was the strangeness of her new surroundings as well as the new smells which aroused in her mild anxiety. It was a good thing that she slept in the same room as some of the children, otherwise she might easily have been overcome with homesickness.

Aunt Frida looked in briefly to see how she was. "Are you still awake, my child?" she enquired kindly. "Of course there are so many things that are completely new to you; but don't worry. Everything will soon fall into place."

As she eventually closed her eyes, Liesel's mind was still full of the many scenes that she had encountered on their journey: the rivers, the cities and the never ending forests and meadows. The sheer scale of all that she had seen overwhelmed her, so that she seemed to herself be just minute. Eventually she drifted off to sleep. Nightfall spread its cloak over the whole of east Europe. Far behind her lay the beautiful city of Kiev, wrapped in tranquillity. Not many miles distant from it was the insignificant little city of Chernobyl.

To begin with the little foreigner encountered more German culture than Russian ways and wisdom. To be sure she did also see from time to time one or two of the pious priests whose practice it was to wend their way prayerfully through the countryside and who were always glad to accept Mennonite hospitality. In addition there were quite a number of gipsy groups in evidence.

One day Liesel met the elderly lady who was their neighbour and who had been in Charkov for many years. "You are a good girl", she said, "so let me advise you that one must be specially watchful on Sundays when everyone is out of the house. Otherwise you will return to find nothing left!"

However, as events turned out there was just not enough time for her to get down to a proper study of the Russian language as had been arranged. The fact was that the little children she had charge of engaged all of Liesel's energies.

The farmer's daughter was particularly struck by the imposing style of the farm steadings she saw. A special feature of their architecture were the lovely Roman archways at the entrance to the farm which were constructed out of the finest masonry. Then too there were the lovely flower gardens and the many different sorts of farm animals. In that region there was a much smaller rainfall than in Germany, yet the Mennonite farmers had accustomed themselves to the climate over the centuries and had succeeded in transforming the Donetz basin into a fruitful paradise. Indeed, the German colony there got on famously with the local Russian people, many of whom turned up to help with the work on the fields or in the stalls.

One evening the young niece turned to her uncle and asked him, "Please tell me, uncle, how did the migration of Germans to Russia come about?"

"I will gladly explain as much as I can about the history of the Mennonite arrivals here," he replied. "I think it is a really fascinating story. As you will be aware, the practice amongst the older generations of the Mennonite groups who held a pre-Reformation faith that derived from Switzerland was that they would not take any oaths or perform military service. As a consequence, other countries would simply not give them refuge, even in spite of the fact that their skill as farmers was proverbial. The background to this hostility was the fact that Europe at that time was divided up into a host of small states which were constantly at war with one another. Naturally they all wanted a well-equipped army.

Liesel nodded. She had already picked up a good deal of information about the tragic persecutions which had afflicted her ancient forebears.

"After Frederick the Great had won the seven year war", uncle continued, "he automatically assumed control of the farmers who had already settled in the lowland marshes where cherry trees proliferated. Of course he was not really at all pleased that they refused to do any military service. However, he had given a guarantee that in his country "everybody had liberty to conduct their lives according to their tradition". Consequently he kept his promise, even although it was a perpetual charge on his budget to do so. It was too much trouble to pursue legal minutiae; and in any case Frederick held the Mennonites in high esteem. However, Frederick's successor proclaimed the so called Mennonite edict in 1789. The upshot of this was that everyone who inherited a farm was bound to do military service. Naturally this caused severe pangs of conscience for farming families who usually had many children. One result of this was that there was widespread need and poverty. Then an unusual set of circumstances came to their rescue.

"It happened that at just that time there was a German princess who ruled Russia. She later acquired the name Catherine the Great (1762-96); but she might just as well have been called the Catherine the Cruel. By means of an officers coup she arranged that her relatives would be wiped out, whereupon she sought to prolong her rule as dictator. The first prerequisite for establishing her reign in this way was that she needed an outlet to the sea."

At this point uncle stood up and went to get a map of Russia. He pointed to St.Petersburg. "Look here in the north was where Catherine obtained her access to the sea. However, it was too cold in the winter months for shipping to off-load here, and in addition it was very remote from the other oceans of the world.

"By contrast here in the south she had the Black Sea where she was however able to drive out the Turks. At the same time, there was the real threat that the depopulated area of the black earth region would turn into a complete desert. How could anyone, especially farmers, possibly be attracted to come here? Now it happened that there was a Russian officer present at a banquet given by the Czarina who had been stationed in the area where the cherry orchards were during the seven year war. He reported that he had met Mennonite farmers there who had created high-yielding fields out of swamps and undrained ground. He was sure that by then there would be far too many of them there. Catherine enquired extensively about their situation, and she then promised them release from military service and exemption from tax as well as providing them with sufficient land in the Ukraine."

"What!" exclaimed Liesel. "You mean to say that they reached their present state of prosperity simply by the good reputation of cherries?"

Her uncle laughed. "No; of course it wasn't just as simple as that. However, I cannot give you all the details of the story. Naturally a delegation of the Mennonites wanted to inspect the land. Prince Potemkin, who had oversight of that region, received them most cordially. Even given the fact that these shrewd, earnest farmers quickly saw through the high-flown rhetoric which the prince used to impress them -you know the kind of flattery that the villagers of Potemkin use-, they were still very taken with the fine quality of the ground and a climate that was mainly southerly.

"Even so it is still not easy to leave one's homeland and set out into the totally unknown. In addition to this, the Prussian administration created enough problems of its own. Above all, when someone takes the step of faith in leaving family, farm and fatherland, it is essential to have an experienced spiritual mentor. Sadly, this was the one person which those who now undertook the trek south lacked."

Liesel commented: "So it's as if the first one dies, the second barely survives, and only the third one makes a living from the land."

"The stream of immigrants continued for several decades," uncle said as he took up the story again. "However, for the later generations of incomers, who soon discovered that the land here was suitable for building on, things did not go so well as with their forebears, because they had to pay tax. Soon other Germans also arrived, both Protestant and Catholic. Thus it did not take long for the German community in this region, if you include those exile Germans who were by then living in the Volga and in Kazakhstan, to total several millions. We have good schools, and from early on we have become respectable Russian citizens. We are confident that the Czar is glad to have us here, and that he will continue to afford us his protection."

There is no doubt that Uncle Benjamin was correct in what he said. Liesel drew comfort from his words.

"I have taken to this place like a fish to water," she wrote home to her grandmother. "It is much more beautiful than Breitenau. Aunt Frida recently said to me, "Liesel, you did well to get out into the world." I definitely agree with her. Who can say whether I would ever have learned a fraction of what I have experienced here if I had stayed at Breitenau."

At that time there was a lively spiritual revival in the parishes in and around Halbstadt. One figure who stood out on account of his attractive personality and positive outlook was the parish elder, Brother Wiens. He was a frequent and welcome guest in the Unruh house, and it was not long before the question of Liesel's baptism arose; for this would have been easier to arrange in Halbstadt than elsewhere. It appeared as if Liesel had little inclination for this move, and Brother Wiens was certainly not the person who would try to persuade her into it.

"A forced Christianity," he declared, "accomplishes nothing. Conviction of this sort must come from the heart."

As a result Liesel had no instruction, an omission which she later rectified as an adult. It is interesting to note from her collected papers how, amongst the jottings, is evidence that even at 70 she was still trying to recollect the 10 commandments and the phrases in the confession of faith.

One of the letters that has survived from this period gives a good idea of what life was like for Liesel as a sixteen year old.

Halbstadt, 12th May 1913

My dear, beloved brother Heinrich!

By the time you receive this letter your birthday will already have been swallowed up in the events of the past. Sorry for the many failed attempts to write to you, but children demand one's constant attention.

Dear brother, you are afflicted with a tendency which is part of my own character, namely, disobedience and anger. Fight against these dispositions as if you were training for the gold medal in a race.

At home here disobedience and dissent are not tolerated, so that everything runs as smoothly and happily as fresh water. The church bells are ringing outside. It is Sunday, and I am looking after the children.

Everything is going well here, and we hope the same is true with yourselves. How is beloved Grandma keeping? Dearest brothers and sisters, learn to be obedient. I know only too well how stubborn I was towards those who were my elders, and I now very much regret my wrong attitude.

I have a completely different outlook on everything around me here, nature, daily life – in fact everything. Whenever I take the children out into the fields and meadows walking, it seems to me as if everything is at its freshest. The birds, the flowers, the grasses: they are all bursting with life. It is a wonderful country.

You would not be able to imagine just how beautifully the birds around here can sing. There is a nightingale in our garden. Just 10 minutes away from our house there is a 'bush', as they call it locally, on account of the fact that this is how they view small forests in the neighbourhood. This is because the trees and shrubs have the appearance of a dense thicket. However, in between these thickets there are plenty of open, sunny playing fields where my friend and I can roam in the sun and enjoy ourselves. Yes, just recently I met a very nice girl of my own age and we have become good friends.

Ach, such is life! I must be ready at all times to roll up my sleeves, wash the children, undress them, and clean up around the house. I must make some more progress on completing my summer clothes. But what do you think about those who must starve because they have been removed from their homes? That is a terrible business! I must draw to a close now, although it would really be no trouble at all for me to continue scribbling like this for a hundred more pages! However, the children keep on interrupting me.

Please give my greetings to all my uncles and aunts, and especially to my brothers and sisters. Lots of love from here, and a thousand kisses from your own Liesel who often thinks about you. Do write soon, won't you?

Liesel

It had already been arranged *in* the interim that Liesel should start her return journey home in the spring of 1914. However, there were two sets of circumstances which delayed her departure. To begin with Aunt Frida was expecting another child, due to be born in May of that year. Secondly, Liesel received news that Uncle Hans and Aunt Julie had left Breitenau, and that the family had sold the farm. Naturally, it made more sense to spend the summer in Halbstadt, and Liesel was agreeable to this. The little life made its entry into the Unruh household soon enough, and the new baby girl, the fifth in the family, was a delightful, cheerful black-haired child.

"We could call her Liesel as well," suggested Aunt Frida, "so that when you return to Germany in the autumn we shall continue to have a Liesel with us."

But before the autumn of 1914 came the summer of that year. Just a few weeks after the birth of tittle Liesel uncle returned home one day in a very agitated state. He reported that in nearby Serbia there had been considerably unrest. The heir to the Austrian throne and his wife had been shot in Sarajewo.

"If Austria now attacks Serbia, then our country will certainly go to the aid of Serbia," uncle added emphatically. "Germany is tied up with the Austro-Hungarian Empire, and she will not be able to remain neutral on a long-term basis; but that of course means war. Liesel, we shall need to organize your exit papers as quickly as possible. Otherwise it will be a long time before you ever get back home again."

Liesel would need to be issued with a new passport, because apparently on entering the country her status was described as "child" in her passport. Or had the passport been mislaid? Who was to blame? These were incidentals; but what huge consequences they had. Before the new forms could be filled in the war that everyone had feared broke out. On the 31st July the Russian and Austrian armies were mobilized. It would no longer be possible to make a return journey to Germany.

Liesel had already packed her case, and she had been prepared for several days for her return home, so that when her new passport arrived she would not need to miss another train. Now, however, on that beautiful warm summer's evening when the news came in about this turn of events, she spent a long time staring out of the window, as she often used to do. She was suddenly aware of just how much she longed to be with her own family, and especially her grandmother and her brothers and sisters. Then a secret fear welled up within her. What happened in a war? Where might she, as a German citizen, possibly wind up if she were detained?

Outside it was very quiet. In that far-off corner there was not a hint of the turmoil that was shaking the whole of Europe. As she stood at the window, Liesel could smell the scent of the ripening corn fields near at hand when the evening air reached her. In fact harvest had already begun on many farms.

At the very time when that young German girl stood in such distress at the open window of a farmhouse in distant Russia, the British Foreign Secretary Sir Edward Grey was watching the lamplighter as he made his way round St. James' Park in London. With an agonized tone he exclaimed:

"The lights are going out all over Europe, and we will not live to see them being relit."

CHAPTER FIVE

"ELIZABETH MUSELMANN, I WILL NOT LEAVE YOU DESOLATE:"

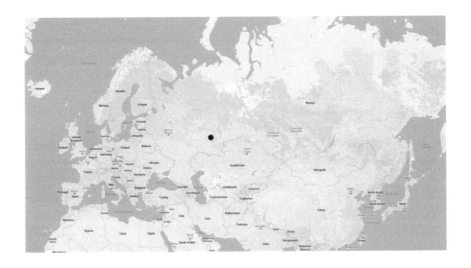

"No-one can be a child of heaven who was not beforehand a child of hell."

Martin Luther

War! War!

"We will not be given call-up papers," said the Mennonite men in the community. "The Tsar guaranteed us freedom from active service in the army, which means at least that non-Germans will be fighting Germans."

Now how were fellow-citizens who were Russians, and who had to enlist, going to understand this situation? Even where Mennonite farmers wholeheartedly supported those Russian women who were working on their own to bring in their harvest, a spirit of antipathy grew between them daily. Bitterness finally gave way to hatred which spread like poison, so that overnight people who had previously got on well together suddenly became sworn enemies.

Uncle Benjamin organized a delegation of Mennonite menfolk who went to St. Petersburg, so that at least gave them a chance to undertake medical duties. Their petition was approved, and due respect was given as always to the exemplary behaviour of the Mennonites. However, the Tsar could not override the wishes of his opponents. On 2nd February 1915 he ratified the sequestration of property. This meant that over one million Russian citizens of German extraction had within a very limited time to hand over their estates. Sermons in German were forbidden. As the Russians were terrified of an invasion by the German army, one could anticipate a lot of violent, criminal activity in the near future.

However, before these new laws became operative, Liesel was arrested on her eighteenth birthday, 20th July 1915. The military police decided that, as a German citizen, she should be sent to the border of Siberia - to a place called Ufa - where there was an area of the country which had also been settled in by Mennonites.

Although it was prudent to anticipate the possibility of internment, the trauma visited on the Unruh family was nonetheless considerable as Liesel was collected from their home and taken to the station. She was the only one taken prisoner in the whole of Halbstadt, and she composed herself with great fortitude. Incidentally she was convinced that this kind of deportation was likely to be short-term.

"You need only count on a few months of imprisonment," said uncle as he took leave of her. "Do not worry! The Germans are victorious everywhere, and soon they will have occupied the Ukraine. Then you can return to us."

Liesel's journey lasted four days and four nights, and she was confined inside a locked goods wagon along with others who were non-Russian. Fortunately it was mid-summer. She sat at the door which had been left slightly ajar. The first stop was at Zaryzin which was to be renamed as Stalingrad ten year later. For many years after that journey Liesel would hear in her dreams the clickety-clack of the railway lines.

Their journey took them ever northwards. In the distance the heights of the Ural Mountains could just be seen. On they travelled, slowly making their way through prairies, beautiful woodlands, villages with broad, dusty streets and lovely, attractive wooden cottages that looked so inviting. Liesel had never imagined that the borders of Siberia, in which they now found themselves, could be so hot.

Setting out from their terminus at Ufa, Liesel was taken by horse and cart over the rolling flat plain to the home of a farming family who had a most unusual speech. Initially she did not understand a single word of what they were saying, and it seemed to be a mixture of Russian and a north-German dialect "Plattdeutsch."

On arrival she was handed a prisoner of war card which was to serve the purpose of notifying her relatives in Germany of her new address. It was her brother Heinrich who preserved it. No one could guess how vital a piece of evidence this document was to become many years later.

It was to be in this new sphere that a tough part of her schooling was to begin for the young girl who had, in many respects, had quite a sheltered upbringing. Her new surroundings made her feel that she had landed in a wilderness. She found it impossible to make meaningful conversation with anyone on the farm, and she was immediately detailed to do the hardest and most menial tasks. Liesel had no doubt that these people were of a very different sort to her kind, sympathetic Aunt Frida.

She was often overcome with terrible outbursts of anger and obstinacy. "No birch stick was considered too thick to test on my backside," she later explained. "Indeed, no swear word was too coarse to hurl at me, even when I did not understand it. They were continually bawling me out for doing things wrongly. The military police used to call in from time to time in order to check that I was still there. Every orphaned child learns very quickly that it is only there on sufferance and that it must toe the line immediately, or else; but in my case I lost count of the occasions on which I was denied even my daily bread."

Finally, she became so indignant with her circumstances that she decided simply to make a run for it, and to take her chance in the city where she might be able to beg for her meals. As she could speak German, she thought that they would surely welcome her into the schools to teach. In addition, she could play the piano, and she felt confident that one of the many musical Russian families would take her into their nice home and ask her to give music lessons.

It was a journey of well over 20 kilometres to Ufa. Very early one morning, Liesel secretly made off from the farm. As the length of daylight in those northern regions is that much longer during the summer, it was certainly well worth her trying to cover that distance under her own steam. She soon realized, however, that she was no walker. In addition, her command of Russian was insufficient to enable her to make herself understood. Wherever she went people turned her away. She was nearly dying of hunger after three days as she had no money, and when she eventually took to the streets to beg for her bread, she was no different from any other female beggar around: dusty, dishevelled and with her clothes in a mess.

There was no alternative: she would have to return. She arrived back at the farm after a long, weary foot-slog more dead than alive. She was greeted with a hail of abuse.

"What do you think you're playing at? We'll be in deep trouble with the military police if they think we are not watching our prisoner!"

The next few weeks were terrible.

One day Liesel had been kept busy in the field hoeing until evening. Thereafter she was to hang up the washing to dry. What happened next is unclear, but the young girl had obviously got on the nerves of the farmer's wife.

"What are you doing just standing there by the washing trough, you cheeky thing?" was her opening salvo.

"Well, I can run away again if I want to!" shouted Liesel back at her.

"That's not right either. The military police might see you!.... Ach, off you go! I don't want to see you again! And make sure that you get right away this time!"

Right there and then Liesel took off into the hinterland, just as she was. Impotent rage, despair and defiance overcame her all at once with such force that she could no longer control herself. She raced into the wood which lay at the foot of the hills. She prayed that she would not meet anyone. Anywhere would be better than here, she thought to herself. She ran until she dropped.

"I'm just an orphan child, someone who is expendable in this world," she moaned to herself. "What's the point of living any longer? Let me sink into deep sleep, not wake up or have to get up again - that is the one thing left to me, and that is what I will do!"

Just then she came to a small clearing in the wood. The moss here was so thick that it was like a feather bed. She lay down on a nice looking patch and drew up her feet towards her as it was already growing damp, cold and dark. Overwhelmed by a sense of misery, and deeply troubled by what seemed to her the pointlessness of her existence, Liesel sobbed her heart out. Soon her face was so covered with tears that she could not open her eyes. Then exhaustion overtook her and she fell fast asleep.

When she came to again she felt that she was being touched by a ray of light, even although her eyes were closed. At the same time she had the sensation of gentle warmth soothing her aching limbs. In the depth of her being she heard quite clearly the words: "Elizabeth Muselmann, I will not leave you desolate." (John 14:18). With a combination of alarm and joy, Liesel realized the presence of a greater reality. She felt herself surrounded by radiant, eternal love; and whilst it made her aware of her many failings, she was far more conscious of being upheld by God's mercy and kindness. Did her parents and brothers and sisters surround her at that moment? Or was it death, that death which opened the door to a new life?

She lay still for a moment or two, quietly taking in the many little noises around her. She heard the stirring of the various animals in the forest; maybe there were even wolves near at hand. She realized then that all her fear and hatred, all the bitterness and despair had been lifted from her heart. She had been touched by the hand of God. For Liesel would never be the same again after that night in the woods of the Ural Mountains. It marked a profound turning-point in her life.

At length she succeeded in opening her tear-swollen eyes a fraction. The moonlight shone down on her brightly, and it seemed to fill the clearing where she lay. As she looked up, she was reminded of how, as a child, the moon's face always appeared friendly. Those were the days when she was warm and secure at home.

Shortly she discerned human voices in the distance. They came nearer, and she heard twigs crackling. Then a lantern was held directly over her.

"There she is," called out the farmer with a note of relief in his voice. He and his wife had spent hours looking for her. The farmer was a man of few words. Awkwardly he fetched a piece of bread from his pocket and handed it to her, and then he helped her to get up off the ground.

"And what do you think we should have said to the military police?" whispered his wife in an agitated fashion. This time, however, the tone of her voice was not unkind. She had a pang of conscience about her treatment of Liesel, and since her young prisoner of war had run away she had had time to reflect on the despair which had gripped her.

But Liesel too had undergone no small change in the interim. Dutifully she followed them back to the farm, and the next day she undertook her duties in a spirit of conscientious good will. Underlying this improved performance was her new found faith that, no matter how lonely she might feel, in the depths of her heart she knew she would never be forsaken. Perhaps inner freedom grows when we lose our outer freedom.

All this time, however, decisive human intervention was near at hand for her; but it arrived from a source that Liesel least expected.

One forenoon a small horse and cart drew up alongside the garden fence. The farmer's wife was working with Liesel in the summer kitchen, and she peered inquisitively out of the door. A tall, elderly man strode purposely towards the house. There was something dignified about his appearance.

"That is Jacob Thiessen," the woman declared. "He is a much sought after person in this neighbourhood. In some way or other we are all dependent upon him. Even the Tartars treat him well. He originates from the Ukraine, and a long while back he took over the inheritance of an uncle who was childless. There is not one of us in the community who has not received some kindness from him, whether in the form of a beast of burden, a tool or friendly advice. Now that we are caught up in a war, we look up to him as the leader of our community. He is a thoroughly honest man who has real strength of character. I wonder what he wants from us."

She dried her hands on her apron and greeted the visitor respectfully on his arrival. Jacob Thiessen asked if he could speak to Elizabeth Muselmann. Then he took the girl aside.

"All prisoners of war have to be taken away from here," he informed her urgently. "They are to be exchanged with Russian soldiers who are presently in German prisoner of war camps. Your name is also on the list, Miss Muselmann. They will call for you within the next few days." The man then drew close to her. "I can only advise you not to go! Not a single person whom I have seen leave this place has ever arrived in Germany. I do not wish to add to that at present; but I will ensure that you do not go."

Jacob fixed his eyes on Liesel with a look of fatherly tenderness and concern. For a moment she averted her gaze to the ground, anxious lest he should become aware of her inner turmoil. When he had broken to her the news that she might soon be away from here and be on her way home to see her grandmother, her relatives and her brothers and sisters, she had fleetingly become dizzy at such a wonderful prospect. He walked over to a pile of birch logs and invited Liesel to come and sit with him.

"I know full well just how you must be feeling," he said to her sympathetically; and then he continued. "In any case you are no stranger to me. I am a relative of your uncle Benjamin's, and he wrote to tell me of your being here. I also grew up in the Ukraine, in Schonau, and I know Halbstadt very well. I went to school there. My last teacher there was Cornelius Unruh, an uncle of Benjamin's. If I had had the good fortune to have been tutored by such teachers, I would have benefited ten times more from my schooldays than I did." Jacob paused for a minute, and then he added: "I am telling you these things so that you may have confidence in me.

"You realize that it is impossible for you to return at this time to the Ukraine, nor indeed could you go back to Germany as long as the war is on. I wanted to make another suggestion to you. I would like you to come to my home as one of my children. This was my first thought when I heard of you being here. Don't worry about anything; I will soon arrange this. In this way you will be in far less danger than you are in now as a citizen of the German Empire."

Then he told her: "I have four daughters of my own, and I am already convinced that they will be very good sisters for you. If this seems acceptable to you, then I will come to collect you next week. In fact," he said turning to point towards the east, "you can even see from here some of the fields in our estate."

Liesel could scarcely find her feet as she followed Jacob Thiessen to his carriage where the horse was stamping its hoof impatiently. She was simply bewildered with disbelief at such a turn of events. She watched him as he untied the horse, took the reins in his hands and bad her a cheerful farewell.

But would this kindly man really come back again to take her to his home? She knocked her forehead with the palm of her hand and rubbed her eyes to assure herself that she had not been dreaming it all. Wow! Life was just great! What on earth had she been thinking about just a short while beforehand when she had wished her life away?

A week later Liesel was taken to the estate belonging to the Thiessen family. Her last few days with the farming couple sped by quickly and pleasantly. In fact the farmer's wife could not get over her amazement that her young prisoner of war was to be brought up as a "lady". The thought of it: on Sundays she would ride over the meadows on a fine, well-bred horse. She would also play the piano and the balalaika with the four Thiessen girls.

THE OCTOBER REVOLUTION

Vladimir Lenin

"Ultimately this is what the command to love means: there can be no strangers in the world as far as you are concerned, only people whose welfare and woes should deeply affect you."

Albert Schweitzer

When Liesel entered through the beautiful rounded archway at the entrance to the Thiessen's state she was both timid and inquisitive. It almost seemed to her as if she was in the Ukraine, for the large farmhouses there were very similar. People were prosperous, but they had a modest lifestyle.

How was Liesel treated by Jacob Thiessen's wife? She scarcely writes anything about her; but it would appear that her relationship to this attractive, but somewhat reserved woman did not result in their becoming very close.

What probably did not help was the convention which was still observed by the children when addressing their parents in the house, to call them by the formal "Sie", instead of the more intimate "Du". This made Liesel's relationship with the daughters all the more important. Their father was quite right in what he had told Liesel: she did indeed get wonderful sisters. Here is what she says herself in a letter which has survived from that period in her life.

Kanjatschapkansk, 13th October 1916

To everyone of my dearest Family!

When I wrote my last prisoner of war card I said that this letter would follow. I wonder if it will arrive. You too are in the midst of war. The name of my address must sound strange to you, I am sure. The farm on which I am living is a very big concern. It would be difficult to imagine an estate of this size at home. For example, there are approximately 2,000 square hectares of land and 150 horses along with assorted herds of cows and flocks of sheep.

Although this estate is not exactly in the middle of Siberia, it is not far away from it. The striking range of mountains in the Urals seems to look down at me every day, and during the summer they are surrounded by a haze of blue mist. Just now the highest peaks have had their first fall of snow. The world of nature around here is simply fantastic. As it is now autumn, the many birch trees look so beautiful with their golden colours. The large farmhouse belongs to a family called Thiessen. They are also Mennonites, and they have taken me into their midst as if I was one of their own. Really, they are just so sweet, and they have shown me so much love and kindness.

Of the seven children (three sons and four daughters) only one daughter is at home at present. The three sons were all called up for military service (what a terrible business this is when Germans have to fight against Germans!). If you try to avoid it here you are immediately press-ganged into fighting. The daughters are still away at school where they get a good education. Their names are Katya, Selma, Greta and Elsa. Katya and I play the piano, the guitar and the balalaika together. As girls usually do, we crochet, knit and darn clothes. We are not allowed to overwork!

I am very happy the way things have turned out for me as a prisoner of war. You must not be in the least worried about me. You have probably also got all sorts of hair-raising stories circulating about war "happenings".

The same kind of tales go the rounds here too, only friend and foe are exactly reversed. Recently an old "babuschka" (which is what they call the old women around here) told me she thought that all Germans had black blood!

I am well provided for with food and drink, and at night I have a lovely warm bed. The soldiers around here would be over the moon if they were as lucky as that. As far as my daily schedule is concerned, I just do whatever needs to be done around the house, and I am more than glad to do my bit for such a wonderful family as the Thiessens. On Sundays Katya and I take the horses for a ride. We travel far over the prairies. It is fabulous! You really have to learn how handle the horses in this region. The thing is that the distances are too great to allow one to break them in on foot. In addition, depending on the weather, you might find that the tracks are too dangerous for carts.

Uncle Benjamin and Aunt Frida are well, I am glad to hear. And what about sweet little Olga who was born after I left? Of course I have not had a chance to see her yet. Who knows how long it may be before I can return to the Ukraine, what with this war dragging on and on! Now they have six children, and I can't go and help them! Uncle and Aunt send me money regularly which means that I can live quite comfortably.

Please send me a photo of yourself. Dear Grandma I hope it will reach me. Oh how I wish I could just see you all again! It is now four years since I last saw my brothers and sisters. Would it be possible for you also to send me a photo of them too? Please write soon and write lots of news!

With heartfelt kisses to you all,

Your Liesel

Just after Liesel had sent the above letter she experienced the onset of her first winter in Siberia. In 1916 it was particularly severe. The entire transport system ground to a halt owing to the continuous fall of snow. The few items of news that percolated through to Jacob Thiessen from St. Petersburg and the Ukraine cast a shadow of gloom. The first waves of starvation began to spread through Russian cities.

As the head of his family, Jacob Thiessen was a wise man and laboured under no illusions. It seemed to him, in the light of his constant observation of what was happening in the political scene, that the murder of Grigori Jeminowitsch Rasputin towards the end of 1916 signalled the advent of very uncertain times. Rasputin, for all his enigmatic ways, had exercised considerable influence with the Tsar and his family. True, there had always been occasions of unrest in such a vast country as Russia and, it must be added, sometimes these revolutions had been justified. Of course it was just as well that Rasputin's influence had been brought to an end; but was his murder perhaps merely the first act in a reign of terror? Jacob asked himself what was brewing. Hunger, war and freezing temperatures. These were not good omens for the coming Spring.

Liesel wrote these words in February, 1917 on the one prisoner of war postcard which she was allowed to write at that time:

I have now been here nearly two years in these wild Siberian plains in the north of Russia. I am grateful to God that my life is pleasant enough, and that is certainly something that cannot be said of everyone here. A few days ago there was at long last a let-up in the terrible winter we have had. For long enough the temperature stayed constantly at or around -27C. The snow fell day after day without intermission. Honestly, you could not imagine what it was like; and for myself as well, it was simply amazing that so much snow was possible.

Then the wolves started coming in from the prairies and they were prowling around us here. At night one could hear them howling. Actually they are really quite shy creatures, but hunger drives them to seek sustenance in the vicinity of humans. At least in this area they do not come right up to the houses since there is a relatively high density of population here.

Whilst Liesel's postcard was wending its way towards its destination in Germany, a bald-headed emigrant from Russia whose name was Vladimir Iljitsch Ulyanov was pacing up and down in his humble dwelling in Zurich in a distracted manner. He came from a good family, and his mother was of German extraction from the Volga region of Russia. The man was well educated and totally fearless. However, owing to the repressive regime of the Tsar he had been forced to flee from his homeland because his ideas were revolutionary. Later on he was to change his name to Lenin.

The young emigrant felt like a caged lion and he eagerly seized on every scrap of news that came out of Petersburg. But now things were beginning to take place there which really demanded his presence; and was he to be prevented from directing those events? The first major incident was the so called March revolution. The Tsar was forced to abdicate. A few months later he and his whole family were murdered.

As far as Jacob Thiessen was concerned there was nothing particularly surprising about these developments; and for the time being no one was shocked by them. As a result the sequestration order, which had been aimed principally against all German immigrants in the Ukraine, could no longer be implemented. One sensed that a coup was imminent, and that the Tsarist family, the Romanovs, which had so much blood on its hands and which had determined the course of Russian history for hundreds of years, would now at length be overthrown.

There was an atmosphere of general euphoria throughout the Ukraine at the prospect of this new set of circumstances. The leading statesman at that time was the Minister of Justice, Alexander Kerenski. He accorded a warm welcome to a delegation of Mennonites in Petersburg, and he promised that they would have full voting rights and representation in the new Russian national assembly. Uncle Benjamin was elected as the leader of the newly formed Ukrainian congress. It all looked as if the long awaited day of freedom and peace was nearer than ever before, and that a new day had already dawned for the largest of Europe's kingdoms.

Meanwhile on the Thiessen's farm the work of sowing the summer fruit was undertaken with a new confidence. At the same time -April, 1917-Lenin made his way through the whole of Germany, with the approval of the Reich, in a sealed railway carriage on his way to Petrograd, which was the new name by which St. Petersburg was now generally known. It was the secret hope of the German army that this city, which was regarded as the military showpiece of eastern Russia, would be completely shut down as a result of the revolution which was about to take place. Then at least it would be possible to achieve an armistice with the Russians. How cunningly it was all planned and set up! Later Winston Churchill was to write about this ploy: "Lenin was smuggled into Russia like the bacillus of some plague."

Just when Lenin was travelling to Russia, the U.S.A. declared war on

Germany. Germany's position looked completely hopeless. As far as the Americans were concerned, their rather sudden commitment in European affairs was one from which they were not able subsequently to break free.

Those Germans who were in Russia then suffered in a double sense on account of these events. Their hearts were torn in two directions. On the one hand they were hated as Germans locally; but on the other hand Russia was their homeland. Oh dear! How would everything work out?

Way out on the borders of the Ural Mountains there was nothing especially unusual, at least in the summer of 1917, to indicate the impending storm. Following this letter of Liesel's, written in the autumn of 1917, there was to be no further regular correspondence from her for a considerable time. Maybe it is a sort of historical law, that those who are most immediately caught up in the great events of a century are least aware of what is unfolding around them.

Kanjatschapkansk, 9th Oct 1917

My dearest, golden Grandma!

Should the peace for which we are all longing be soon established, I shall patiently await an opportunity of at last coming home to see you all. A war which had a beginning will also have an end. Don't give up!

In the evenings we have no lights, and so I can only complete my letters bit by bit. Today I received your card written in May. It took a whole half year to get here. Many thanks for your news. You too are enduring this terrible war.

I can imagine you enjoying grapes at home just now, and you will soon be making this year's wine. It all comes so vividly to life for me when I think about these things! I dream about pears, plum cakes and peaches. There are no fruit trees here. There is an apple tree in the garden, but that is quite exceptional, and it does not bear any fruit. Most people here cannot imagine what fruit trees look like, just as I can hardly visualize what an orange tree or a date palm looks like. Recently I was describing to some people locally the way apple trees blossom. They looked at me as if I was telling them some kind of fairy story...

This is the start of my third winter here. What lies ahead? Winters in this region usually begin as early as October, and mostly without any warning, literally from one day to the next. Meanwhile, I have become very well acquainted with the strong, Siberian character of Jacob Thiessen.

It is ages since I heard anything from Uncle Benjamin or Aunt Frida in Halbstadt. Apparently Uncle was chosen to work in the ministry at Petrograd; but you can never be sure what to believe, or if it is true. In spite of all the good things that I enjoy here, I just long to be able to see you! Homesickness never leaves you, even when strangers treat you well. It will certainly be New Year before you receive this letter, so this brings you warmest greetings for Christmas. Oh how I wish that there might be peace by then,

With thousands of loving greetings and kisses,

Your Liesel

Another winter drew near, and still there was no sign of peace on the horizon. All of a sudden the revolution took place, and at such speed that Lenin, who had once more been forced to hide himself on account of his radical speeches, scarcely had time to throw away his wig and the spectacles he wore. The October uprising swept through the land with such momentum that, for days on end, Lenin and his conspirators were never out of their clothes. As Liesel was to report later on, it must have been a tremendous upheaval.

Of course, as everyone knew, Lenin had appeared on the scene to champion the cause of freedom and justice. He made his aims quite clear. He wanted to put an end to all the plundering that was going on, and he was intent on destroying the interests of capitalism. He expected a new humanity to arise from the dawn of socialism.

Then, without warning, Russia was overwhelmed by disaster. Had expectations been too high? Of course. The farmers wanted land; those in the starving cities cried out for bread; and everyone wanted peace immediately, and freedom too. Instead of these things, however, what people got was an outburst of unparalleled terror. Jacob Thiessen, that quiet, serious observer of all that was happening, might perhaps have repeated this statement: "Where people recognize no accountability before God, they will very soon treat human beings the same way."

A workers' and farmers' State was declared; but what emerged in practice was civil war. It is likely that Lenin, who was well-versed philosophically, had plenty of reflections to make about the theory of socialism; for he could hardly have foreseen how rapidly revolution and counter-revolution activate each other, nor have imagined the depths of brutality to which people can sink.

It was particularly in southern Russia that the civil war resulted in terrible brutality. Liesel was consumed with anxiety about the Unruh family who had become so dear to her. It was painful to hear of groups of Red Guards who marched from village to village singing and burning houses down on their way. Always on the look-out for counter-attacks, they would make off with whatever they wanted.

In that winter of 1917/1918 the Thiessen household could once again hear the howling of the wolves echo across the vast distances of the Siberian plains. What was far worse, however, was the bellowing of the "Reds" and the screams of those they were attacking. Then there was a prisoner named Machno who had broken out of his jail in Siberia. He was responsible for one bloodbath after another.

One evening just before winter, Jacob Thiessen returned home sorrowfully after attending a secret meeting of Mennonite elders. In a hoarse voice he related how Brother Wiens, whom everybody loved, had been murdered in a horrible way and his body had been thrown into a mass grave. He was scarcely able to speak about other atrocities about which he had had been informed. "We are still protected by the remoteness of this locality and by the harshness of our Siberian winter," he continued. "However, we shall have to prepare ourselves for the worst. As soon as the frost releases its grip on the ground, we shall have to bury what we can. Oh Russia! Our dear motherland, now hacked to death and red with blood - you never deserved such a fate."

CHAPTER SEVEN

EXPULSION

Dawlekanowo

"Without God anything goes."

Fyodor Dostoyevsky

The Thiessen family observed the Christmas season of 1917 in a subdued mood, occupied as they were with anxious forebodings. It would scarcely be appropriate to speak of "celebration". Snowstorms swept around the house and stalls, and they also silenced the unfamiliar noises for which everyone listened when the wind was quiet. Although the Gregorian calendar had been introduced into Russia in February of 1917, the nation did not celebrate Christmas until New Year, so that it was doubly necessary to be on the watch. There were no Christmas carols, and Katya did not touch the piano so as not to cause any upset.

"Pray that your escape might not happen during winter," whispered Jacob Thiessen to himself from time to time as he reflected on this word of Jesus, particularly if he received disturbing news from the neighbourhood. "Those who live in The Holy Land know nothing of Russian winters; yet this saying matches perfectly our time and circumstances."

45

"Dear Thiessen, the Bolsheviks will not touch you," a poor, stunted agricultural labourer said to him one morning. "You have helped us all. We will tell them: 'Father Thiessen has always paid us our due, and he has been a good landlord'."

Jacob Thiessen looked affectionately at the old, worn out man; but then he shook his head: "Those who lead this people lead them astray, and those who are led by them are swallowed up" (Isaiah 9:16).

A flicker of anger passed over the old man's eyes. "Do you mean to say that the new leader of the revolution is a devil?"

"My brother, I was only quoting a verse from the Bible!"

"From now on it would be better if you did not quote from the Bible, Jacob Thiessen. It is no longer appropriate."

Shortly afterwards all hell broke loose.

It was during a night in February 1918 that the beautiful old farmhouse was overrun by hordes of Redshirts. They made short work of reducing it to dust and ashes. Doors and windows were smashed in, the floorboards were ripped up, and they robbed and plundered all that came into their hands, creating chaos and mayhem throughout the whole property. The occupants fled outside on a plain sledge with curses and whiplashes spurring them on. Once they had done their worst the evil animals fled into the prairies. Like huge torches, the burning farmhouse and barns lit up the night sky as the refugees fled for safety. What had taken decades of careful, painful work to build up was destroyed in a matter of a few hours. That winter the wolves had plenty to eat. The Thiessen family was given emergency accommodation by friendly neighbours. Seven people now had to live together within one room which had no heating. Then the hunger began. There was a crumb of comfort, however. At least their own fields were accessible from where they now were. Hopefully come the summer they would get food and warmth.

The family bore up well in the face of such adversity. They were all grateful that at least they were all still alive together. By his presence in that little room Jacob Thiessen ensured that everything ran smoothly and harmoniously. Over against all that was mean and vile in humanity during that terrible era, one saw in him the triumph of integrity.

A letter from Liesel has survived from those years. In the light of the fact that there was virtually no exchange of mail between Russia and Germany during that turbulent period, it represents something of a rarity. A soldier who had been released from P.O.W. camp forwarded the missive.

Dawlekanowo 25th January 1919

Dear Brothers and Sisters! Dear Grandma!

Presently there are many German prisoners of war who are travelling through our vicinity, so I am entrusting to one of them this letter in the hope that it reaches you. Would you able to do the same in reverse?

It is now more than a year and a half since I had any news of you all. I sometimes ask myself if I would ever reach home if I were to entrust myself to the kind of P.O. W. transport they have here. I would not risk it. In any case, the trains in this region only go a short distance at a time. Meanwhile, we have been enduring temperatures of -35C. Not one of us has good, warm clothes. Even if I am dying from homesickness, I shall simply have to put up with it here for the present.

I am afraid I can only give you sad news from this end. You simply would not be able to imagine what atrocities have been committed here, and in many other places in the interim. Every day some other foul deed is carried out. I truly believe that the 30 years' war was tame in comparison with what is happening now. One estate after the other is seized and then they just smash it to pieces. The houses have all been ruined. They have no roofs, windows or doors, and the floors have all been ripped up.

The sheer injustice of it all cries out to heaven. Even the dear, dear people under whose roof I am staying just now (I don't need to spell their name) have nothing but what they stand up in. Our beautiful farmhouse was completely destroyed a year ago, and there is not a sign of life on the whole farm. We guess that even the rats do not find anything more to eat there. To begin with it was neighbours who took us in; but now we are moving about from place to place.

I was ill for quite a long time with rheumatism, and I was also troubled with bad teeth. However, I do not have money to visit the dentist. Just now my teeth are not giving me so much pain. I cook and bake for the family, and I make do with what we have. I cannot say how grateful I am to the Thiessen family that they did not put me out in the street when they were robbed of all they had.

On 9th June, 1918 I was baptized here in the Mennonite church in Dawlekanowo. To be honest, baptismal instruction was simply out of the question. I went of my own freewill. I am conscious of a lack of self-control in my life. It is lovely to see how caring each member of the Thiessen family is for the welfare of the others. I hope to God that all the hardship which I have experienced in my life as an orphan will serve to make me more mature and help me grow in faith.

But how are you, my dear Grandma? And how are all the rest getting on? Have you all survived the war? Oh dear, I wish I knew an answer to this mystery as to why I have to spend so much of my life in unfamiliar surroundings. Please excuse the poor quality of the feather I am writing with and the tatty piece of paper, but there is nothing better. We make our own ink.

Once again it is Saturday tomorrow, a day I just hate. The drunkards behave like mutineers, smashing everything to pieces, plundering and murdering at will. One thing at any rate, there is practically nothing left for them steal! I am taking the risk of writing this, because none of them can understand German, should they confiscate this letter.

I send you my heartiest, most tender greetings, from one who is banished from you, but still longs so much to be with you at home,

Liesel

"Four black angels were riding over Russian soil," someone said at that time. "Their names were plunder, devastation, hunger and death. They are turning holy Russia into a hell."

An organization that was particularly feared was the Cheka (An abbreviation for Commission for Opposing Counter-Revolution, Speculation and Sabotage). There was a civil war in process, which even the great Lenin himself was not remotely in control of. Anyone who dared to defend themselves against injustices was shot out of hand "like ducks in a pond" (Trotsky). The pressure to surrender anything that was demanded of one became oppressive. Hunger and sickness were the result.

Then cholera affected the whole area around Dawlekanowo and Ufa, so that no one dared to leave their house.

However, where there is danger, courage also comes to the fore. Thus it was that, one day Jacob Thiessen's youngest son Wanja (Hans in German) stood at the door of their house. At long last one of his sons had been freed from military service. It took Wanja a lot of time and effort to find his relatives, but at last he was able to run them to ground in a different regional authority.

There was great joy at the homecoming of this son and brother. First of all, however, Wanja wanted to look over "Chutor", which was the name of his family's farm. He decided to make a thorough investigation of what could be done. He was young, healthy and energetic. He was definitely not going to let his property simply lie and rot. He was quite determined that he would find a way forward.

Wanja had to travel the whole distance on foot because there was not a horse to be found anywhere. When he reached the farmhouse, it was in much worse shape than he had feared. Whilst he was looking round the ruins he was noticed by members of the Cheka who were drinking vodka behind a low wall that had become blackened with smoke. They recognized him as the son of the owner, and that was enough for him to be arrested and sentenced to death.

It was really a kangaroo court. As they could find no suitable wall against which to place him for a firing squad, the execution of this "plunderer" was to take place in an open field by simply shooting him through the head. Wanja later told how, under the circumstances, he was amazingly calm. When it comes to the bit, it is surprising what resources one can draw on. These bandits had clearly drunk too much and, in addition, they had used up nearly all of their ammunition. Somehow Wanja had managed to hide the last three of their bullets in his thick, wiry hair.

As the execution committee debated ways and means of acquiring more bullets, Wanja made a dash for it. Tearing himself from his captors he ran headlong into the fields as if his life depended on it. What certainly helped to save him was the fact that he knew every nook and cranny in the surrounding countryside. As he later recounted, he set off in that instant like some reckless adventurer, and this gave him courage.

Making its rickety way over rough ground in that area just then was a broken down old carriage pulled by a scraggy horse. It was driven by an elderly priest who was being carried along by a poor nag. He was sitting on an upturned wicker basket. Even then priests tended to be relatively sheltered, although most of their possessions in their churches and homes had been plundered.

The bearded old priest was really startled when he was suddenly confronted by a seemingly unkempt young man. Wanja made himself known, and asked the priest if he would give him transport.

"I cannot hide you on my little wagon," demurred the old man. "Look, they have also left me with little more than the clothes I stand up in." Gleefully he lifted his long robe to prove that he had nothing on under it. "How fortunate that it is summer. I must shortly ask some friends for a shirt and trousers." Then he added, chuckling happily, "Do you know what we're going to do? I shall sit on your back, and you will be my seat as it were! My robe is big enough to hide us both."

They jogged along like this in tandem and, although it was not the most comfortable way to travel, their sense of humour carried the day. They had just got used to their routine when the bandits jumped out onto the track in front of the horse and cart, blocking their way.

"I have nothing more to give you," the priest stated quite calmly. "And I cannot stand up any more as I am too old."

"'We are looking for Wanja Thiessen, father. He has escaped from us. We sentenced him to death, and he broke loose. Have you seen a young man anywhere on your travels who is on the run?"

"Wanja Thiessen? Yes, I recognize the name. In fact I did see a young man over in that direction running across the plain. If you hurry you will catch him."

The old priest pointed in the opposite direction. The bandits rushed off plainly very satisfied with this information. Soon this unusual vehicle had crossed into a different regional authority where the danger was not so great. Wanja arrived safely at the house where his relatives were staying, and he was immediately hidden in the underground cellar. The priest received a pair of trousers from Jacob. Both men were chuckling because they adhered to the statement in the Bible which says: "Whoever has two shirts, let him give one to the person who has none."

Wanja had to spend three weeks in his hideout in the cellar before the coast was clear again. When at last he ventured to step out into the open, his brothers and sisters pulled his leg: "You look like a seed potato." Wanja entered into the fun and replied: "You witches have fed me as well as Hansel in the fairy tale! But now I am free, and I know that with each other's help we will be able to fashion a secure future."

However, instead of that a new threat to their lives emerged. To be sure, the cholera epidemic mercifully left the Thiessen household unscathed, but now typhoid was rampant, and in a particularly virulent form. In such close quarters -the family had recently been enlarged to eight members after Petja was released from military service- three of them went down with the illness. It was Liesel who suffered the worst.

"I felt the illness coming on beforehand," she wrote later. *"Suddenly I was afflicted with serious bouts of depression, which is something I never usually have. I was just knocked out, and had not the least spark of energy. I felt so ashamed, and indeed I could not understand myself. Then the fever itself hit me. It got so bad that at one point no one could believe that I would see the light of the next day. I never had such terrible pangs of homesickness, and I really thought that my dazed state along with the dreadful depression were harbingers of death itself."*

Liesel took the whole winter to recover from the typhoid, and during that time she was faithfully cared for by those girls of the family who were still present. At long last when spring came, her health improved rapidly.

It was an unforgettable experience for the young, homeless girl when, one morning, she was able to set foot outside the house. It had already passed from winter to summer, for the seasons in Siberia are sometimes relatively free of transition from one to the other. Liesel paused and took in a deep breath of the lovely fresh air. She was still a bit unsure on her feet, and so she leaned against the wall of the house. The shrubbery had turned a light shade of green, and above her the clear sky was a wonderful light blue. All things considered, it was great to be alive! To listen to the birds singing, to feel the warmth of the sunshine, and to enjoy the scent of the passing currents of air - it was as if she had come alive again.

But what a shock she received when she happened to catch a glance of herself reflected in the glass window of the low wooden house. All her hair had fallen out, and all that was left was a thick layer of black down covering her skull. Her features appeared pinched and sunken owing to the grey pallor of her face, and her eyes stared out of dark sockets.

"I can scarcely appear in society looking like this," she thought to herself dejectedly. "Look, my beautiful, healthy hair! And now I look like a bald old lady. I hope I don't meet anyone. I must quickly find some material with which I can make a wig." However, there was someone coming. It was Wanja who was returning from having collected water. He approached young Liesel gently and, as though he had read her thoughts, he said to her cheerfully: "Your hair will grow again, and it will have a lovely sheen. How many lovely things you will see with new eyes when the summer is really here!"

Uncertain and shy, and not a little confused, Liesel turned to him. What did he say? The warmth in Wanja's eyes seemed like a shaft of that wonderful light which had shone around her and had touched her life that unforgettable night in the forest, when she had heard those words: "Elizabeth Muselmann, I will not leave you desolate."

Suddenly a feeling of happiness filled her being. It was a sensation which she had not experienced before. Wanja took her gently by the hand and led her back into the house.

"DO YOU KNOW WHAT IT MEANS TO BE DESTITUTE?"

Ural Mountains

A kulak said to his neighbour: "You have only a small patch of ground!". His neighbour replied: "Yes, but I have lots of sky above it!"

A Russian saying

Urter - Tau by the Urals, summer 1920

Dearest brothers and sisters! My dear Grandma!

Today is Sunday, and at long last I have some time. It seems as if the civil war robs one of everything, including time! Within the space of two years we have had to move seven times. Each time we have been driven out and forced to flee.

On account of the fact that many Germans from the Reich are returning home, I will try to give this letter to someone in the hope that it will find its way to you. It is useless attempting to post it.

I have not heard anything from you for years, and when I see these Germans

53

going it nearly breaks my heart. However, I do not have a brass farthing to my name so how can I possibly travel? But there is also another reason.

Recently I got engaged to Hans Thiessen (usually we call him Wanja). Hans is the youngest son in the Thiessen family. He is two years older than I am. We are very much in love. However, as a family, circumstances drive us here and there, so we still hope to find a place of our own; but for now all we can bank on is "today". Just at present we are staying with relatives and we have to live and sleep in one room: the parents, two sons, two daughters and me.

It is very hard to adjust to the thought that I may well have to stay in Russia for the rest of my life. Truly I love my Hans more than anyone else; but I also love my home. As of today I simply cannot imagine growing old and grey here. But then perhaps events have come to the point where the very possibility of growing old and turning grey is excluded. Such is the net effect of the great Utopia. And they want to make "new people" of us all by such a philosophy! What a laugh! As if it were so simple...

There have been the most far-fetched rumours about Uncle Benjamin circulating here. One was to the effect that he had been shot, another that he had been abducted, and yet another that he was in prison either in Canada or Moscow. It is years since we had anything like reliable news. Everything is passed on by word of mouth and then of course you have no way of knowing if it's true or not.

Just now, because it is summer, we can always find something to eat. The question is, what will it be like in winter? If they rob us of all we possess once more..! We are using the time now to salt away what we can. Recently we found an old piano on our former estate. Apparently the thieves did not know what to do with it. Now we are storing all our grain seed in preparation for the winter sowing.

Liesel

The last few weeks before their wedding were an anxious time for the young couple. In the first place, all their efforts to get the old farm into some kind of running order proved fruitless. Eventually Wanja got a job as a clerk in the regional office. For the time being a wedding was out of the question as the cramped conditions in which they stayed made a room of their own impossible.

In the autumn of 1920 the family was driven out of their lodgings yet again. They found temporary accommodation in the small town of Dawlekanowo. It was a place with which they were slightly familiar from earlier years.

Liesel's next letter derives from the winter of 1920/21 which resulted in widespread hunger. It even came by post which was an improvement.

The winter here is the worst so far. The conditions are appalling. We are still staying with Wanja's parents. It is quite pointless to get something started on our own, as we are forced to work hard in collective farms. Our old farm is just lying fallow; and that contributes daily to our hunger. It is a case of maladministration, and it is a disgrace! We are made to shovel snow for hours on end, day after day in places where no one ever walks.

For several weeks the temperature held steady at -30C. When there is no wind, conditions are manageable and one can easily endure the cold. However after Christmas we had the "buran", which is a form of snowstorm. Wherever there is a "buran" there is always loss of human life. All of a sudden it turns dark in the middle of the day. You cannot tell if it is swirling snow around you, or whether snow is falling in addition to the wind. It was literally the case that we could no longer see our hands in front of our faces. You could imagine what the end of the world might be like one day. Anyone who happens to be out of doors at the time has no way of knowing if they will get back home. Very near to us two women froze to death. They were travelling from town back home. Just as they were about to make out their houses in the distance the "buran" started. They attempted to ride the last stretch at full tilt. However, when the "buran" had died down, their families rushed outside to search for them. They discovered their bodies scarcely 10 metres away from their home. One woman was completely frozen, and the other was frozen up to her waist; she died shortly afterwards. The wolves were making attempts to seize the horses. These normally reserved animals are undoubtedly very audacious this year. Being crazed with hunger, they have no fear. Our neighbourhood is relatively well inhabited, so that we can actually see them from the window; but they would not really attempt to break into the dwelling places.

Wanja and I are very happy - at least as far as present circumstances permit. I love my Hansel very dearly, and I know that he feels the same way about me. I would not lose him for all the world; but I must admit that it is a high price to pay. The fact is that, in feeling like this, I am bound to say "farewell" to you the more time goes by. When I think about that, I begin to cry and I cannot write any more. Hans must not see me like this, for it would hurt him.

Liesel

Then in the New Year of 1921 Liesel wrote as follows:

...During the day we are outside now as we have more work than we can cope with. In the evenings we sit in the darkness. If we are fortunate the moon shines, but its light is not strong enough to allow one to write letters. Sometimes we put kindling in the stove so that we can at least recognize what is essential.

Last winter seemed to drag on forever, and it was really awful. For nearly a year now I have been sleeping on the floor without a mattress. However, one is so tired that you sleep in spite of such conditions.

Since yesterday it has been possible to till the ground. Hans and his brother Petja plough our field when they are not working in the collective farm. We hope to be able to sow and harvest at least something.

We have the impression that there is less unrest amongst the people at present, so perhaps this dreadful civil war in nearing an end. In the previous year the mobs of Bolshevik wreckers spoiled every field which had been freshly sown with grain, completely overlooking the fact that they themselves also have to eat the same bread as we do. Recently a Tartar said to us: 'I always used to think that even the devil himself could not destroy such a lovely, imposing farm as yours; but that is just what the red-shirts achieved when they plundered, scorched and burned your property.'

I am giving this letter to a foreigner who will post it in Germany. The longing for you will never leave me. Sometimes it is hardly noticeable, then at other times it is like a restless urge. If you are still alive, please do not forget the one who writes to you from the East,

Liesel

It seemed like a miracle to the young engaged girl when, after nearly four years, she received her first letter from Germany in the spring of that year. The letter was from her Grandmother.

The old lady described what had happened during the war, and also how things were shaping up after the war. She told her about what happened to Liesel's eldest brother, Christian. He had died quite unexpectedly just after getting married. Her brother Heinrich had also got married, and he had settled down in Bavaria. All her uncles had returned from the terrible war relatively unscathed. Uncle Hans and Aunt Julie had taken over the running of the estate at Hohebuch in the north of Württemberg. Uncle Benjamin and Aunt Frida had managed, with the greatest of difficulty, to travel back to Germany via Moscow.Presently they were staying in Karlsruhe with Aunt Frida's sister Johanna; they all arrived safely at their destination. The family had now grown to eight children.

Grandma could write nothing positive about the post-war era. The German Reich were forced to pay huge reparation costs, and there was a steadily rising number of unemployed. Although in fact the worst of the hunger had been kept at bay, what really depressed people in general was the very bleak prospect for the future.

"It looks as if things are in a mess politically in Germany," Liesel said to her father in-law. "The French have got Alsace, much of the Saar region and large stretches of the river Rhine have been taken, and now a corridor to Poland has been opened up between East Prussia and the rest of the Reich. The revolution apparently spread to Germany, but its effects were not so serious as they were here. The Emperor lives in exile in Holland. Uncle Benjamin has formed a commission in America which is charged with reporting on the desperate situation facing Mennonites in Russia."

The first thing that brother Heinrich's lovable young wife did was to make up a parcel for Liesel and send it to Russia. After a long while it actually arrived, and it created scenes of unprecedented joy in the household.

Liesel wrote this in the early part of the summer in 1921:

My dear brother Heinrich!

Your parcel has arrived, and it seems like a miracle to us. Now I can make my Hansel some cocoa! And writing paper - how wonderful! I will gladly use it to write to you! ... After years, at long last some news from you! Your tokens of love touched me deeply. Sometimes when Hansel is away I just feel so desperately lonely in the midst of this huge outback of Russia. It would be a terrible pity if my letter never arrived, for writing paper is such a luxury, and there would not be the ghost of a chance of getting some like this here.

Do you know what it means to be destitute? No, you do not know.

I cry a lot when I think of our dear brother Christian who has gone home to heaven. I never had the opportunity of seeing him again. It will be a hard time for our young sister-in-law Gertrud, now that she is without a husband and has no children.

Once again all the menfolk are away having been mobilized. There is a rumour that there is war with Japan. Under these circumstances, we women must do the work of the men, and this appears to be the case throughout the whole of Russia. We have to fell timber.

On one occasion my sister-in-law Selma and I were arrested. I was in the process of leading our horse with a sledge full of wood back home when an official ran up to us panting. He tore the reins out of my hand, and shouted that we had stolen the wood. In fact we had simply taken it from our own trees. After a night spent in detention we were set free; but our supply of wood had vanished in the meantime.

Recently the horses ran over me after I had fallen backwards out of our rickety old wagon. By good fortune I fell full length the right way between the wheels so that by and large I was able to stand up afterwards not having suffered a great deal. The others were all frozen with horror and, when I stood up, they swore it was a miracle. Last summer the hay wagon, which I had loaded, overturned on to me, and I was buried underneath it. There again I came to no harm.

On another occasion we ventured into our wood one night in order to "steal" our own timber. We had truly not a qualm of conscience about that because the trees and all the wood are ours. One should not really think such thoughts; but then everything was taken away from us so unjustly. Well then, whilst we were unloading the timber, a branch rolled on to my foot. I was admittedly unconscious for some minutes, and my foot was swollen for several weeks; but nothing was broken, and everything is once again back to normal.

I have almost forgotten how to speak the German language ...

Cordially

Liesel

Fortunately Wanja came back home in the summer. The war against Japan had not yet started. In the meantime, Lenin had promised all young couples from a farming background that, in the event of their getting married, they would be provided with some land of their own, and they would also have an opportunity of owning their own house. Thus it was that Hans and Liesel decided to marry in August 1921.

Liesel writes:

Dawlekanowo, July 1921

When I take in the fact that I am to get married with virtually nothing to put on, then I realize the full extent of our poverty here. What dreams about marriage I had as a child! I was going to get married in a white bridal dress with a veil, accompanied by a joyful crowd of brothers and sisters and bridesmaids. There would be music and flowers and lots and lots of cakes! Instead of all that, the one shirt I have consists mainly of patchwork! Our bread will last only until Christmas, and there is no more salt left.

0 Russia, Russia - what have we come to! You have no idea what life is like here. In fact we are happy if we have a bit of dry rye bread. Our hands too have become so used to menial, coarse work that they are not sensitive enough to write properly. We are thankful if we are allowed to work with plain, ordinary things, especially if they do not then straight away steal what we have made! The rinderpest which found its way into Russia from Asia has carried off the last cow. However, we do not give up. The civil war is not being fought so cruelly now. Lenin has promised that whatever we earn over and above our dues we shall be allowed to keep. We are relying on that !...

Hans and Liesel were married on 18th August 1921 in the little

Mennonite church at Dawlekanowo. The text taken for their marriage was from 1 Chronicles 17: 16ff

'Who am I, O Lord God, and what is my house, that you have brought me thus far? ... For you, my God, have revealed to your servant that you will build a house for him ... Now therefore may it please you to bless the house of your servant.'

And indeed the young couple got a small wooden house in the vicinity of Dawlekanowo. In addition, they received some land, two chickens that had been stolen, two cows and two sheep. Wanja planned on buying beasts of burden during the winter in Siberia, because, in time of war, there were sure to be good bargains on the go.

This is how Liesel described her wedding day when she wrote to her Grandmother:

It was not easy for me that none of my own family were able to be at my wedding. I would so readily have been a happy girl if you had all managed to come! And of course we would gladly have had wedding photos taken, so that we could have sent you one. However, that would have cost us between 14 and 18,000 roubles! Prices here are rising astronomically, and of course we simply could not afford it.

After the wedding ceremony we had a modest supper. Then the youngsters amongst us had a happy time until the morning. You have no idea what times of real happiness and pleasure we can have here in spite of our many hardships. Katja, my oldest sister-in-law, had some bridal jewellery of her own tucked away which she willingly lent me. My mother-in-law gave me a table cloth. In fact she had prepared a beautiful dowry for each of her four daughters, but she was only able to rescue what she had hidden. The youngest daughter is to be married this summer. The Thiessens are wonderful people.

Now the parents are planning to take a room in the town as from this winter, so Hans and I will be alone. Dear knows what all this winter will bring. I have no more warm clothes to wear. I plan to take some of the wool off one of our sheep so that I can knit myself a warm undergarment. Maybe I can also earn a bit more by spinning, and I have also learned how to mend shoes. You cannot buy anything at all round here, firstly because there is *nothing to buy, and secondly because we have not got a rouble.*

No matter - happily we are able by means of such odds and ends to ensure that our life together is not spoiled. We are happy together; we are healthy and we enjoy working. Every day we find something we can laugh about. Just as long as we can both bring in sufficient to eat, and also give us some warmth, then we shall be quite content with that.

My parents-in -law also send you, dear Grandma, their warmest greetings. This comes to you with all my love,

Liesel

Hans himself also added his own contribution to this letter. It is written in great capital letters, and obviously the young man spent a long time over it. He wrote it from Urter - Tau on 27th September 1921:

Dear Grandmother!

Please do not think too hardly about your new grandson on account of the mistakes that I make in this letter. The German language has always been unfamiliar to me, even although our mother tongue is the dialect of Plattdeutsch. Here we always speak Russian.

My wife wanted me to introduce myself to you in this letter. It was a great pity that none of Liesel's relatives managed to come to our wedding.

Thanks be to God, we are all healthy and alive, but life today is different to what it was formerly. Frankly, it is sometimes difficult to make ends meet, and we are always very thankful simply to have our daily bread. I can assure you that no one could begin to imagine just what painful effort and constant hard work goes into providing the bare essentials of life unless they have had to live that way themselves. Our work is paid by means of things that have been confiscated and other irregularities. As long as this continues, we do not have the least hope of a brighter future, no matter how we work ourselves to the bone. We dare not even contemplate the winter ahead. Just now the number of those who are starving is rising daily.

Your new grandson, Wanja Thiessen

All the hopes which people had set on Lenin's reform measures came to nothing when the winter of 1921/22 set it. Then there was raging famine. "If only we had the chance to be human beings again," Liesel wrote in a letter to Germany. "The trouble is that we so quickly revert to a state of barbarity, acting like animals, if there is nothing to eat. It is really terrible."

The crop failures of 1921 and 1922 brought cholera and typhoid in their wake. Liesel was once again brought low with typhoid, only this time not so badly as the first time. It was during the year 1922 that her relatives in Germany were making strenuous efforts to obtain exit papers for her. Here is her reply:

I am very sorry that brother Heinrich and Uncle Benjamin have gone to so much trouble in order to secure exit papers for me. However, I am now married. My mother-in-law told me: "You can go; but Hans must stay". But how can I be happy without my Hans? And then again, it would be impossible for me to return. Nonetheless, I shall collect all the papers, and when we are over these bad times, then we shall both visit you.

In her last letter of 1922 Liesel wrote:

Sometimes I dream, like a silly goose, of a nice piece of chocolate or something else that is sweet, some days, when hunger is very severe, the desire for something like that is so great that you wonder if you can contain it. At night one dreams of such delicacies as grapes, peaches or even some mouth-watering roast duck.

Nevertheless, there were more things than just hunger for Liesel to write about that year:

At the moment we are having something of a revival in this part of the world. More than 300 Orthodox Russians have gone over to the Russian Baptist church as the result of one sermon. This happened just recently. People are coming from miles around, and there will be more big meetings tomorrow. Unfortunately my Russian is not good enough to make it worthwhile for me to follow the sermons and to travel with the rest to Ufa. However, Wanja is going. The Russians are basically a religious people, so it will not be possible to completely subvert their beliefs. That is basically why we believe that things will eventually turn out alright.

LENIN'S DEATH

Russian Children

"Is there anything of greater significance in someone's life other than their destiny? Yes, the unshakeable courage with which it is borne."

Johann Wolfgang von Goethe

The civil war came to an end.

In spite of all the desperate need that came in its wake, there was an almost audible sigh of relief all round. To be sure, the ravages of hunger continued to be felt far and wide, and there seemed to be an epidemic of theft; even the fields were plundered at night.

Liesel wrote to Germany:

We have to interrupt our sleep every night, in order to safeguard our rights.

In fact travelling by horse and cart had now become dangerous as they had heard reports of people being assaulted in broad daylight. Liesel was always slightly nervous when they made their once weekly visit to her parents-in-law on a Sunday.

But it is certainly a relief, she added, *if you are not accosted daily by soldiers who threateningly demand your last supplies of corn and turnips. We had to conduct a lengthy campaign to keep our Sundays free. However, we finally regained our rest on that day as the commandos who supervise our work also decided to take that day off.*

Outside of the hours which they had to spend on the collective farms, the precious time in the short summer months were full of intense activity for this hard-working young couple. In every sense they had to make hay whilst the sun shone, for there was simply no one who could lend a hand with the work in the stall, the house, the garden and the field. Hans was forced to empty the harvested wheat on the living room floor for there was nowhere else for him to put it, and once again the wheat seed was carefully hidden away.

A letter from the following winter runs as follows:

Urter Tau, 30th January 1923

At long last I can get round to writing. The things that we were giving away are ...now out of the house, and I have put fresh whitewash on the walls of the room. We begin to feel more human now. Sometimes last summer I used to think to myself: 'Really, to imagine that Germans are able to endure this kind of existence!' It was a terrible mess.

However, now everything has once more been put in order. In addition, I now have the wife of one of the Tartars helping me. Her husband gave her permission. Of course, she does not understand very much about the German way of going about housework; but she is willing, she can carry wood and water for me, and yesterday she even baked some bread for me for the first time, and that is a great relief for me. Wanja has travelled to Siberia, beyond the Urals. At present he can buy cheap horses there, and he took wheat with him as a means of payment. At this time roubles are being counted even in millions. He hopes to be back in roughly three or four weeks. It will certainly be very cold for him on this journey, but during the summer we cannot afford to take a single day off. If everything goes well, we should be able to plough properly this spring for the first time in years.

...Every now and then I have to stop writing because I freeze even with furs around me. There is a 'buran' raging outside, although it is not one of the worst. We will manage somehow. We still have wretchedly poor windows, and so the draught blows out the candle-light. Of course, even if it is was available just now, people would not buy glass as it is so prohibitively expensive. No one thinks of counting in thousands anymore; prices are reckoned only in millions.

...We keep asking ourselves exactly how we are going to get through this year. People are going about just like shadows. Sometimes I think that they are no longer like human beings at all.

...Whilst Hans is away I occasionally lie on my bed and cry. I say to myself, "I want to go to Germany; that's all I want." But then when he is back home again, I recollect that love endures and bears all things, and that I belong to him. So for this summer we have just set ourselves to work, work, work, so that we can make the journey to see you, and be with you all to celebrate Christmas together.

...Now it is after midnight, but the 'buran' is making such a noise outside that sleep is impossible. Maybe I will lie down next to the oven in a little while.

...If I can ask one favour of you: please try and send me some seeds. There is nothing to be had here for a garden, absolutely nothing,

Cordially

Your Liesel

Sadly there was a poor harvest in that year once again, which meant that Hans and Liesel could not afford their intended trip to Germany.

I am not going to give up hope, Liesel wrote after the harvest, *that I shall have a chance of seeing you especially, my dearest Grandma, on one more occasion. Now that it is summer our parents are here, and Elsa my sister-in-law is also here. It is really good to have them. Katja my sister-in-law gives piano lessons in town, and Selma mends shoes and sews. When Father Thiessen is around, it never crosses your mind to complain about anything.*

The spring following that year (i.e. of 1924) brought a special joy. After three years of marriage, Liesel was expecting a child. The very idea that, come the autumn of that year, she might possess something in a foreign land that belonged totally to her filled the young wife with great happiness. The beginning of that spring seemed like a fairy-tale to Liesel.

However, before that event came about, another happening took place that was to have permanent effects upon their lives. On the 21st January, 1924 the celebrated and ailing leader, Lenin, died. He had recently turned 54. He was forced to leave all the projects which he had in mind unfinished. It was cold comfort that he died a natural death, an ending which, in those times of murder and corruption, was by no means a foregone conclusion.

It was Lenin's belief that a new society could emerge in Russia only after the rotten edifice of the Tsarist regime had been swept aside. He wanted to pursue his campaign against need and poverty, so that the peoples of the world might enjoy a comfortable life. Lenin had scant respect for the considered wisdom of the centuries, or the many lessons of history. Perhaps he also realized that he did not have much time left. His aim was to initiate a well-structured, planned economy which would be centrally organized from Moscow. However, it must be said that, however gifted Lenin might have been theoretically, he had little insight into the practical problems of running an economy. In fact when he finally admitted that the ultimate incentive for the successful transformation of society was the self-interest of the individual, it was already too late for him.

Many of the things that happened turned out contrary to what he had actually wished. It was a tragedy. Right to the end he fervently hoped that the revolution of Marxist-Leninist teaching would bring about a new man. Indeed, most Russians believed in him, persuaded as they were concerning the better world order which he had spoken about.

"Clear light, total freedom, property for all", are alleged to have been Lenin's last words. Instead of that came something entirely different; and, unwittingly, Lenin had himself prepared the way for it. He had ushered in the dawn of Stalin's era. Initially nobody was really aware just how diabolical a personality Stalin was.

It was a good summer, and Liesel wrote home enthusiastically about the bumper harvest that they could expect, as well as the fields of sunflowers which were ripening in the warm winds. Naturally she spoke of her own joy in anticipating the new baby. She also wrote about a threshing machine which had been acquired by the combined efforts of the collective farmers, and of how easy it made the work of obtaining the grain.

Liesel worked hard on the threshing floor right up to the last day of the harvest. She was in wonderful health physically. The harvest was much better than expected. They could confidently look forward to better times.

But suddenly they were assailed by one disaster after another. Stalin ruthlessly imposed his will in the sequestration of every private property. Hans and Liesel had scarcely got their harvest safely gathered and stored when the militia hounded the young couple out of their home without any notice. Once again they were reduced to snatching a few of their bare essentials, and making off in a small covered wagon.

"It seems as if we shall just have to get used to this routine of being hounded from one place to the next," moaned Wanja as the two of them wandered to and fro in the neighbourhood seeking a place where they could make a new beginning. As he tried one more time to gain a sympathetic hearing at the regional office, this was how he was answered:

"Wanja Thiessen, you and your wife were capitalists and Christians! Now Stalin gives the orders! Think yourselves lucky that you were not put against a wall and shot!"

Liesel began to feel the first gentle birth pangs. "At least Mary and Joseph had an end in view when they set out as refugees for Egypt!" she sighed. "But quite possibly we shall not even have a roof over our heads when the baby is born and winter sets in."

"What a mercy that the weather this year is so mild," Wanja replied. "They will have to give us somewhere to stay. After all, the Russians are especially fond of children - don't worry about it!"

They found an empty schoolhouse in the adjoining village which had also been extensively plundered. The village brigade allowed the young couple to spend the next few weeks there.

As with every other deserted building, they found that the schoolhouse had no doors or windows, the floorboards had been ripped up, and all the ovens had been stolen.

Wanja immediately set out to find an experienced Babushka (Russian midwife) amongst the few inhabitants who were still living there, who could attend Liesel at this time. There was indeed such a one, and moreover a mother whose heart was in the right place. That was particularly important, because although Liesel had been present as an observer at several births before, she soon realized that her own delivery would be a very painful one. At long last, after many trying hours, the baby, a little girl, was born. It was 28th October 1924.

All their worries and cares fell away from them as the young parents took their healthy child in their arms. Now at last, Liesel thought to herself, I shall be able to sink some roots in this inhospitable area.

"What name do you wish to give to your child?" asked the Babushka in a friendly tone.

"It should be called after the name of my old Grandmother in Germany"· Liesel replied. "She is nearly eighty, and if things remain as bleak as they are at present, then she will never see her great-grandchild. So at least she ought to have the joy of knowing that there is a little Magdalena here - that is, if she ever gets the news!"

On the very next day the first flurry of snow blew through the scantily covered window. Shortly thereafter there was a bitter frost. It was impossible to find a serviceable cooker or stove anywhere, so Wanja constructed a stone fireplace instead.

Liesel had been considerably weakened on account of the difficult birth, and soon she began to cough and run up a high temperature. There was no doctor, but all the symptoms showed pneumonia. The next thing was that she could no longer breast feed her child and, although the Babushka did everything she could to help, even the baby began to show signs of illness. Some weeks later it lay lifeless one morning on its little bed of hay. Her small face seemed so tranquil.

"She has gone to the angels in glory, where she belongs," sighed the

Babushka tearfully. "What place should such a heavenly being have amongst us on the face of this earth, so full of horrors? But God knows, no matter how tiny they may be, they still take your heart with them, even mine!"

At that point Liesel was so under the weather with fever, that she did not immediately notice that little Magdalena had died. Naturally Wanja was fearful for the welfare of his wife, and many a time he paced nervously about the room as he sought to do all he could to restore her health. Without telling Liesel he buried his child in good Russian soil. "What have things come to," he asked himself, "when a father is prevented from making a little coffin by sheer lack of wood and nails?"

It was only after many weeks of that bitter winter had passed that the poor invalid recovered her strength once again. Wanja was particularly solicitous in his care for Liesel at this time of her loss and weakness.

"I will be satisfied with nothing less than seeing you fit and well once more," he announced to her with such conviction that Liesel took heart from his positive outlook. Liesel thought of her plucky Grandmother who herself had had to experience the death of several of her own children; and then there was her own mother, Anna, who had died and left seven children orphaned. She wanted to show patience and fortitude in the face of what had befallen her, so that her husband would not have to bear a greater load of sorrow. It was this brave spirit which really turned the tide for Liesel, giving her command of her situation. This was to prove providential, for the coming year would bring them new depths of sorrow.

Once more the narrow little room of their parents in Dawlekanowo was their salvation. Stalin's measures of "purging" the populace, which were directed against the farming communities in particular, resulted in terrible atrocities. In the event, those who were of German extraction were doubly the object of hatred. Instead of things getting better they got far worse.

So it was that, after a restless night, Jacob Thiessen announced in a decisive voice one morning: " It is clear to me that, although our folk have lived in this land for centuries, it is no longer possible for us to call it home. Even although I am over 70 years old, yet there is no other way for it: we must emigrate."

"WE MUST GO! ANYTHING TO GETAWAY FROM HERE!"

Church of the Merciful Saviour, Belozersk

"I flit silently from one population to another like a shadow, and I wait quietly beside them all. No one sees me, although they stare at one another and nod their heads, as if they knew I was there. The unborn and the dead, the greatest and the least in the land all know me. I am Hunger."

Laurence Binyan

Alright then, let us emigrate; but how do we go about that? And where are we to go to?

After a considerable interval of time, Jacob Thiessen learned that many people in his own Ukrainian homeland had attempted to emigrate, and even to flee the country. It was impossible to go to Germany, mainly because the terms of the Treaty of Versailles had brought about very harsh economic conditions in the country. In addition, the German people had not yet recovered from the effects of the rampant inflation.

"The fact is," declared Jacob Thiessen, "that most of Europe has been crippled by the war, so there is no point in thinking about remaining in Europe." As far as they had been able to discover, Uncle Benjamin Unruh and his friend Abraham Friesen had managed to establish some form of contact in Canada. This had apparently resulted in a scheme whereby the Canadian authorities had been willing to receive Mennonite refugees from Russia.

However, the practical question remained as to how so many impoverished people would be able to raise the large amount of money required for such a journey. Eventually the national railway company, Canadian Pacific Railroad, stated its willingness to accept these refugees against the pledge of respected public figures. The sum of one million dollars was submitted as a guarantee, which at that time represented a considerable sum. Even the German Reich made the sacrificial donation of several million Reichsmark in order to assist in the rescue of Germans who were stranded in Russia. Nonetheless, in view of the thousands who wanted to leave Russia, these donations seemed like a drop in the ocean. Liesel's next letter, which arrived safely in Germany in spite of the adverse conditions of the time, has this to say about her own circumstances:

Dawlekanowo, 3rd December 1925

The parents have definitely decided to go to America. They envisage no future prospects here. It is particularly hard for them. All our goods and chattels will be sold, but in spite of that we will still not be able to raise enough money for our fares. Wanja and I will not be able to go with them straight away. In the south of the country many Mennonites have apparently been allowed to leave without any difficulty, and they have even been given credit. By contrast, we here in the north have had one lot of trouble after another. In addition to that, we are constantly being driven from place to place, without so much as a chance to settle in anywhere.

As soon as our situation is clarified, we shall let you know. We simply cannot give you any definite time for our departure, as the local travel documents have to be purchased here with substantial backhanders. Apart from that, there is not a road out of this locality that is open at present. This year we have had too little frost, as a result of which our horses continually get stuck in the mud. This presents a real problem for us, as we cannot even carry two hundred weight of goods through this quagmire to our place of work.

In fact just a week or so ago all our hopes of emigrating missed going up in smoke by the merest hairsbreadth. What happened was that Papa Thiessen was ordered to report to the regional office. As usual under such circumstances, Hans represented his father. After all, in such weather conditions, an old man would hardly reach Ufa. The reason for this command was that, by Stalin's orders, all former members of the German Reich were to be banished to Siberia. Hans refused to hand his father over to such a fate. Eventually he said to them, "I will go in his place."

However, when the news got out locally that Hans was to be banished to Siberia, all the farmers and the people from the communities round about united as one man in their protest against such a move. There was a huge outcry about the matter. "We simply will not allow it," they proclaimed, "that someone should be sent away from their family into exile. If you do this we will kill every one of you." In the end they did actually let him go.

In the meantime, Hans had made further enquiries about getting emigration papers, but he had no success. Recently when he called at the regional office, they started taunting him by suggesting that, like many others, he should try to get into Manchuria by crossing the river Amur. He should try it, they sneered; perhaps he would get rich once again over there.

Christmas is approaching. Is that not really meant to be "Peace on Earth"? There is not a sign of that here. Our greeting of peace to one another is: "Brother, sister, don't lose heart! Don't through away your confidence! ...
"

Indeed, that was the news that had somehow filtered through. Many of those who had been Kulaks, and were now exiled, along with private farmers from every background and religious confession had attempted, either in groups or individually, to flee across the Amur River. It was reported that a community of Mennonites who had trekked into freedom together had actually succeeded in crossing the Amur River one bitter winter's night when there was low cloud and more than 50 degrees of frost. Under these conditions they had managed to navigate 56 sledges over the ice of the frozen Amur and so reach Manchuria. Months later, and in some cases years later, these intrepid refugees managed to reach the American continent after unspeakable hardships. Who can begin to describe the spiritual and physical extremities which occasion such desperate journeys?

Some members of the extended Thiessen family did indeed manage to reach America. However, no emigration papers were given to the erstwhile "profiteer" Jacob Thiessen and his son Hans.

Subsequently Liesel decided to see if she could reach Germany, even if it was on her own. She figured that it would be easier for her to get Hans out of Russia in this way.

She wrote:

> To be honest, parting with my dearest Hans, my Wanja, is unbearably hard for me; it is really a nightmare. Twice before I have experienced that, when you are separated under these circumstances, you do not have a speedy reunion. Thus when I first left Germany, I thought: 'This is only for a year or two!' And here we are fourteen years later. Then when I left Aunt Frida, I said to myself, 'It will just be for a couple of months', and here it is ten years later...

Although there is no specific account of it in Liesel's writings, it would appear that in the following winter Mama Thiessen fell fatally ill. It is clear, however, from what she later recorded, that Liesel attended faithfully and with great devotion to her mother-in-law right up to her death. This of course prevented her from visiting Germany. With the advent of spring, Liesel was pregnant again.

Here is her letter:

Urter-Tau, 16th April 1926

Dear Grandma!

> I want to write to you now before we have our huge thaw here which signals the start of hard work once again. Up until now we have had nothing but winter weather, and that means non-stop snowstorms and frost. What can I say? The last winter was hard and bitterly cold. Hans' fingers got frozen whilst he was bringing in the wood, and now he has no more feeling in them. As for snow, you never saw so much. In fact it fell to such a depth that many of the little huts had real difficulty in keeping their chimneys free of snow.

Notwithstanding all that we send you our hearty greetings for Easter. We heard that you already celebrated Easter on the 4th April. Here it is not until 2nd May.

America seems to figure in every conversation that we have. There is nothing more for us here, and so far it has not been possible for me to travel to Germany.

Now I am pregnant once again, and expecting the baby by the end of July. No woman who is pregnant is allowed out of the country, so that means that the earliest we might be able to travel would be in October. We just wonder how we will manage with Papa who is no longer able to endure the cold here. Of course there is not the slightest possibility of our parting from him. What they are demanding for passports now is quite wicked. We have even heard that, in spite of giving huge sums of money to the officials, some people have still not been given their passports.

You would not believe how risky life is here in every direction.

God's hand is more comprehensively in control of affairs than all our thoughts and conclusions. We simply trust that He will direct our path for the best ....

Your Liesel

That summer Liesel gave birth to a little boy after which their plans to emigrate were given new impetus. However, their efforts to get passports were frustrated at every turn. In her next letter Liesel describes the situation:

Dawlekanowo, 7.Dec. 1926

Dear Brother Heinrich, and my dear sister-in-law Friedl, whom I have not yet met!

...Where do I begin? What is the first thing that a mother should write? Of course I must start by telling you about our new baby. Yasha entered this world on the 11th August. He has been named after his grandfather Thiessen. Yasha is the Russian form of Jacob. The delivery was very painful. To begin with it appeared as if he was dead; but by means of some

74

gentle shaking, and with the aid of some cold water, we soon got him to announce his arrival!

Four days after his birth we were once again due to be thrown out, having to leave everything behind. However, on account of the delivery they allowed us a postponement of 14 days.

Hans is presently transporting vodka, 60 kilometres there and back. The authorities have no wish to employ native Russian folk for this task as, even when it is diluted, they are never reliable enough. When the weather is reasonable Hans is away for four days, but when it is bad he may be as long as six days away from home. He earns between 30 and 40 roubles a week from which the price of fodder for the horse has to be deducted. Naturally, since he is seldom at home he also has to buy something to eat whilst he is on a journey. The bread is very acid tasting here, and it is ages since we could even contemplate buying clothes or washing soap. Recently we all went to see the doctor in preparation for our departure. My lungs have become somewhat weaker, and I am not allowed to breast feed any more. All the papers relevant to boarding the ship, entry permit and financial guarantees have been processed in Moscow. The only thing that is needed are our passports from here onwards, and they are not easy to acquire. Of course if you are prepared to pay a substantial backhander, then you might get what you want; but we are in no position to engage in that kind of bargain just now .

...Meantime, I really want to let you know something about our little Yasha. He is a sweet little child, and already we can detect that he has a musical aptitude, apart from which he seems to be well endowed in every sense. He has a very healthy appetite, and he is growing at quite a pace. But what kind of future faces him? Often little Yasha and I have shed tears together.

How will things develop? We just do not know. If we do not get our passports, there will probably be no alternative for us but to go to Siberia and lease some land there. In this place you can work yourself to the bone without making any progress at all...

...Our schools look so miserable just now! Up to now we had a central school, but they have made a soviet-style school out of it. Two years ago all teachers were forbidden to attend church services. Preachers, conductors and choir members were all made redundant. Pictures mocking God and

the Bible hang in the school corridors. From an early age children are taught that all life and being develops spontaneously from nature. When I think of this kind of teaching, it really makes me shudder for the future of my child. If it should happen that we could indeed get passports from Moscow, there is only one thing for it: we must get out of here, anything to get away from here!

However, in the meantime we have staying with us here in the house an eighty year-old uncle, one of Jacob Thiessen's brothers. Until last year this dear old man was pretty sprightly and he helped us a lot. He also told us many stories about what Russia was like long ago. However, now that he senses that his end is near, he sits quietly at home waiting for eternity. His composure is such a blessing for us.

Dear Grandma, you are also in your eightieth year, and the thought that I might not see you again affects me deeply. Would it be possible for you to have another photograph of yourself taken? We also wanted to try and get one taken of ourselves, but first we had no money, then no clothes and finally the roads were impassable...

...Presently our elder in the church is David Isaac from Halbstadt. I knew him there, but he did not remember me anymore. He told us a lot about life down south, and it seems that things have gone even worse there than here. Now and again we meet in each other's houses. We stand in great need of this kind of fellowship..."

The old uncle died shortly thereafter, but father Thiessen stayed in the family. Wanja was able to get a wooden house which he made into a comfortable dwelling for them. *"This is the first real home we have had tor a long time,"* Liesel wrote in her next letter to Germany, *"and we are very grateful."*

From this point onwards there is no further mention made of their leaving for Canada. The intended trip never came off. Jacob Thiessen never pursued matters that could not be fulfilled. Instead he devoted himself more than ever during this stressful time to his active little grandson Yasha. In no time at all the two "Jacobs" were virtually inseparable.

Meantime Wanja and Liesel both had to work in the collective farm.

However, they were allotted a portion of the nearby glade. It was 5 metres wide and 40 metres long, which were the approximate dimensions of a very large, narrow living-room. They must have wept with joy over this small piece of land.

Suddenly life became very threatening again. Stalin closed all the churches, and they were put to use as grain silos or club-houses. Christians then arranged to meet in secret in their houses.

Although Liesel's relatives, especially her brother Heinrich and his wife Friedl, faithfully despatched parcels to her in Russia (the lists of contents have been preserved), it would appear that during the fateful year of 1927 not one arrived at its destination. In her next letter, which did arrive in Germany, Liesel gives this vivid description of her situation:

Dawlekanowo, November 1927

...Sometimes we do not understand why God allows us to pass through certain circumstances. I must confess that this continual turmoil in my life has thrown me off balance spiritually. My dear Hans is a much steadier person whose sure grip on life inspires confidence; and to that extent he is an exact replica of his father.

...For long enough Dawlekanowo is supposed to have been elevated to the status of a city. If this became a reality we would have our own regional office. Ach, so many ideas and promises! Frankly, one no longer believes them anymore. The latest news is of more plundering and robbery. Instead of things getting better, they only get worse.

...There is such a flood of refugees here just now you simply could not imagine such a mass of humanity. Some of them want to find a way to the south of Russia. Others have come from there and they say that terrible things are happening in the region of the Volga. Yet others are intent on travelling to the interior of Siberia. There are trainloads of pilgrims who are making the journey to Amur right on the Chinese border. All of them want to try and start a new life somewhere else. At the moment all the talk is of the Caucasus region owing to the fact that getting to Canada is somewhat problematic. Some have even mentioned Cuba! What a list of wanderers: Tartars, Jews, Mennonites, Protestants, Catholics, Armenians, Ukrainians, Kirgizians - all of them straining, jostling, rushing, travelling, fleeing. It would really

take your breath away just to watch all this going on. I wonder if such a movement of peoples is a sign of the end time? Believe me, these are the kind of thoughts that come to one.

...Now here comes my little Yasha. He is occasionally rather restless, and I often have sleepless nights with him. Last week he started to walk properly for the first time; but as he is now 15 months old that is a bit late. However, he was very sick this spring, and it lasted some three months. There was a bad dose of dysentery going the rounds. On two occasions Wanja and I stood by his crib and we were convinced that the little one's life had come to an end. It was an anxious time, but we thank God that he has been given back to us. He is now able to make good sense with his words. He is a happy, alert little boy who is very musical. He is quite content singing children's choruses half the day, the very ones which our mother taught us, and which I now sing with him. He is our sunshine, and he brings us so much joy every day. I wonder if you heard that we had a little daughter three years ago who died not long after she was born? It is years since I heard anything from you. It is a great loss for Yasha that he has no little sister to play with.

A year later Liesel wrote this next letter in the winter of 1928:

Dawlekanowo, 1st December 1928

My very dear Heinrich and my dear sister-in-law Friedle, whom I have not met... Thank you, yes, thank you a hundred times! At length after years one of your parcels has arrived. I am sure that it represents only a fraction of what you have sent. All the same, just when things were at their lowest and we seemed to have no strength left to even seek a way forward - that was just when your gifts arrived, and that was when hope revived and we found new courage. Oh how true it is that afflictions teach us to pray. That has been our experience. It is honestly no exaggeration to say that, without your parcel, we would not have survived. Yes, and afflictions also teach us to be thankful, and because of that we do not give up. Every ray of sunshine fills us with deep joy, and every happy day amounts to sheer blessing for us. Each evening in which we have been able to eat sufficiently we consider ourselves to be fortunate. Our little boy is so happy in spite of everything, and his cheerful face is a tonic for us even although his clothes are just rags.

Praise God, we have been given a small piece of land. Without it we did not know how we were going to survive. Hopefully we shall be able to get a crop of potatoes from it. We hope that our labours will not be ruined by theft, and that we shall be able to make at least a reasonable harvest from it. I am afraid that these are the kind of thoughts that beset one continually owing to the fact that, humanly, we have no way out of here.

Sometimes we did lose heart completely; but then, even in that extremity, we somehow believed that God would allow us to go on living because he always gave us something to eat and drink. You have to have such moments to recognize how precious life is.

Last year we were not allowed to start harvest before October, and as it is very frosty by then we lost a good percentage of our potatoes and grain. This system of collective farming is such an unbelievable fiasco that no people can be expected to survive it.

Apart from potatoes, everything else grows very poorly in this region. You really have to be fortunate to achieve something as definite as a harvest. Last year we had to substitute red turnips for bread. I cooked the turnips and then rubbed them on the grater, after which I added to the turnip gratings a mixture of barley malt (if I had any). This was then left to simmer near the fire, or sometimes I put the pot right into the flames. It is ages since we had a proper oven. How true it is that necessity is the mother of invention. At such times we often thought to ourselves: this "bread" is simply staving off death by hunger. In any case, it invariably gave us bad stomach pains. However, the pangs of hunger were even more powerful; and when it came to the bit, one just took a hearty bite! ...

I wish you a good New Year, and that you will have a better harvest than we have had. We had to bring the grain home on sledges, and even then it was only good for feeding the chickens. This is the reason why so many farmers are completely bankrupt, because they cannot fulfil their target. They are all facing exile in Siberia. The injustice of it defies comprehension...

...At the beginning of last week we had virtually nothing. No wood, no potatoes, no flour, nothing. But now the week has ended, and somehow we still managed to get through it. We don't even think about clothes and washing powder. We have received notification of another parcel from you. Will it ever arrive? I don't trust anyone around here anymore...

CHAPTER ELEVEN

EXILED TO SIBERIA

Trans-Siberian Railway

"You must be in despair in order not to despair."

Soren Kirkegaard

A few months later -about springtime of 1929 - Wanja Thiessen was woken up one night by the strange smell of something burning. When he opened the window he saw that smoke was billowing from the western side of the house. That was not the side of the house on which the cooker was situated; but the house was alight! It only took Wanja a second to sum up what had happened before he seized little Yasha who was sleeping in the washing basket, and then he fled from the house yelling at the top of his voice.

They were just in the nick of time, and they were scarcely able to rescue the most necessary items and throw them, along with such food as they could salvage, out of the window.

Little Yasha cried as the flames crackled and spread. There was simply no point in trying to quench the flames as they had got such a hold.

Their little home, which they had only recently been able to make comfortable, was burned to the ground. Was it a case of arson? It was futile to speculate about the matter.

In the immediate aftermath they were given temporary shelter in the home of some hospitable and friendly neighbours. Eventually Hans was able to obtain another wooden house that had become free, mainly on account of the fact that Liesel was awaiting another child. This house was also in Dawlekanowo, and it was not far from the little plot of ground which was so vital for their survival.

Eventually, on the 19th September 1929, Yasha's long-awaited little brother was born. Yasha was three when this happened. He was named David in memory of his grandfather Muselmann.

At that time mail deliveries to and from Germany once again became very erratic. However, there is one postcard, filled with closely written handwriting, which tells of how Liesel was getting on at this time. Sealed letters scarcely ever reached their destination during those years.

> *Thank God we are all healthy, and we are more or less able to get sufficient food to survive on. Our little David has already shown that he is a happy, cheerful little fellow, and he is well able to call out, "Mamamama". We get so much pleasure from him, but especially from Yasha. Wanja is always able to find some work...*

These were the last lines that Liesel wrote from the Urals to Germany. The Stalin era was truly terrible. Every day there was some report about the "Black Raven", a vehicle of the secret police for detaining people, and how it had rounded up some poor farming family who had been transported to Siberia. As there were hardly ever any motors in their vicinity, Liesel shuddered when she heard the sound of any vehicle approaching during the night.

"Yes, I'm afraid our turn will soon come as well!" Wanja sighed one day. "When they come for us, it is sure to be at a time when the ground is still frozen to a certain extent. So let's get ourselves ready!" Provisions were made ready in sacks, although they knew that they could not take too much because there would be a tight control of all that they had. They were aware of that.

It was during the night of 1st May, 1931 that the van stopped at the Thiessen's house. They were informed that Wanja and Elizabeth Thiessen were to be evacuated to Siberia.

"Just don't touch my father", barked the son full of bitterness. Wanja was a courageous and battle-hardened man.

"It wouldn't be worth our while", mocked the brigadier. "He's going to stay with his daughter; we'll leave him with her."

They were already aware how these abductions took place. The van taking the evacuees went to the railway station at Ufa. On arrival they were all summoned to a roll-call, and thereafter they were all herded into animal wagons.

Whilst the young couple gathered together what few possessions they had, Jacob Thiessen stood in the doorway. He stood erect, silent and calm. Fate had dealt him yet another hard blow, but it had not broken him. From his expression at that moment, it appeared as if inwardly his gaze reached out beyond the temporary nature of events in this world. Yet he was intent on not making this parting any harder than it already was. In any case, it might be that their exile would only last a couple of months. It was unthinkable that any State could survive such gross maladministration in the long term.

"May God protect you!" he said earnestly.

As she gathered her two little sons, drunk with sleep, into her arms, Liesel called out: "Father, does God keep his promises?"

"Most certainly he does!"

"My child, you must rely on them anyway, however dark your path may be."

"But are not his ways and thoughts so much different than ours?"

Jacob Thiessen said nothing. Instead he gently blessed the two little grandchildren, who were by now fast asleep again, by stroking their heads with his strong, practical hand. As he touched them they gave the merest shiver in their mother's arms. Then the van disappeared into the night. The old man remained behind alone. How long would it be until the first tint of dawn would redden the sky?

"Lord, as the burden is not getting lighter, strengthen our shoulders to bear it!" he prayed silently.

He did not know (nor ever did find out) that on this very night a little boy was born in the midst of the vast Russian continent whose name was Mikhail Gorbachov.

Bit by bit the far off peaks of the Urals emerged out of the twilight. The birches, fir trees and pine forests all seemed to wave their branches at the departing family as if taking leave of them as they sped away on their journey. Soon they were no longer alone. At the embarkation point in Ufa there was already a queue of people who were making final preparations for departure.

The family spent six days and six nights travelling. The packed goods wagons wound ever onwards towards Siberia. Yasha and David were the youngest passengers on board this train. However, in spite of the unpleasant circumstances, they were very good, and their uninhibited chatter brought many a shaft of humour and light relief into the sombre and embittered atmosphere of the wagon. Every now and again there were interminable stops, and the little five-year-old Yasha showed his curiosity by asking endless questions, which were doubtless not always answered to his entire satisfaction.

Their destination, as later became apparent, was Anschero-Sudschenk. This was an up-and-coming industrial centre which received city-status at the time when Wanja arrived there. It was situated on the borders of the Taiga, between Novosibirsk and Krasnoyarsk, not far from the border with Mongolia. Although it was on roughly the same latitude as Hamburg, its climate manifested typical extremes of temperature associated with that region of the continent. The main industry here was coal-mining. This strenuous labour demanded a large workforce. In addition, there was also ancillary work in the production of pit-equipment.

"I must see to it that everyone pulls their weight in this country," Stalin had once declared, and it was quite clear in this part of Russia that this was beginning to manifest itself in the steadily increasing rate of technology. Evidently the many exiles here could at least point to some fruit for their labours.

They arrived when spring was turning into the summer, the best time of the year, for the days were noticeably longer. Thus it was that the newcomers saw a far less forbidding aspect of inner Siberia than they had imagined beforehand. All the same, Hans was immediately arrested and put in prison. Frankly they had to allow for that as the hatred against German farmers had really increased considerably.

Initially Liesel, who was almost beside herself with indignation, was placed in a camp with her children where she was set to work with the upkeep of the premises. Little David, who was a favourite with everyone from the start, could accompany her to work. On the other hand, Yasha, who was nimbler and stronger, kept on evading his mother. However, as there was a fence surrounding the camp, Liesel was not worried about him, the more so as there was always someone about who would see him.

Nonetheless, on one occasion Yasha remained lost right up to the end of the day, inspite of a thorough search by all those in the camp. It was a very warm summer's day, and after her shift, Liesel raced frantically round the perimeter of the camp to see if there was any hole in the fence through which he might have slipped away. As it happened, she did indeed come across a defective section of the fence where a child might easily have crawled out.

Should she go and inform the station management committee? She was reluctant to do that on account of the fact that they had never had positive experiences in relation to these people who were adept at being inhuman. In her despair she softly whistled to a Russian whom she saw passing by that section of the fence. There was a distinction then between "human beings" and "soviets". The man in question had a friendly face, and he instantly joined in the search. In fact he soon discovered the youngster fast asleep in the hollow of a field nearby, and when Yasha saw his mother earnestly looking for him by the fence, he quickly scurried back through the hole with a shout of recognition.

"I am sorry, Comrade, that I have nothing to give you as a token of thanks", Liesel whispered to the friendly Russian. He simply shook his head, and said with a smile: "Be happy that I didn't keep the child! He is a wonderful little fellow".

When Wanja was released from prison after several weeks, he was temporarily blinded owing to the fact that he had been kept in conditions that were dark and damp. Plainly he had also suffered considerable physical and emotional damage. He did not reveal if he had been tortured. Wanja was unable to bring himself to say much about these terrible weeks, and he certainly would have found it impossible to engage in normal conversation about such depths of human depravity. Many of those who suffered with him were subjected to torture from which they never recovered. They formed part of the six million people who, between 1931 and 1934 died because of starvation and other repressive measures.

The family were given miserable accommodation from which they were soon ejected. During these early years of their stay in Siberia they were continually subject to homelessness, starvation and abject poverty.

No further letters arrived in Germany. However, a letter from Liesel to her sister-in-law who had emigrated to Canada has survived, and it originates from these early days in Siberia. Its contents are very moving.

Anscherka (a suburb of Anschero-Sudschenk), Christmas 1931

Dear step-sister Greta!

The five Dollars which you sent as a Christmas present have arrived. May God repay you for this kindness!

If this letter ever reaches its destination, please answer me, so that at least I shall know if any of my letters is reaching its destination.

...Now I must let you know that Yasha was very ill, and we think it might have been measles. He yearned very much for his Grandfather Jacob who of course was so far away. In the evening he used to nod happily at me and then at little David. He had such a bright countenance and shining eyes. Eventually, he stood up in his little bed one day, clapped his hands

and looked upwards, as if he was expecting to see something wonderful. He had always longed for a drum. He then began to shout and cheer at the top of his voice, but after a minute or two he suddenly collapsed. His eyes and lips were closed for ever.

The following day, after dark, we laid our child to its final rest. Meantime Hans had become blind, and the other German men are all away at work. The Tartars are very superstitious, and in such circumstances immediately suspect the plague. I had no one at all to help me, and it was with many tears that I laid my child in the Siberian earth. Yasha was just over five years old, and such a lovely boy.

The next day my dearest little David lay in bed full of red spots, but apart from that he did not look in the least ill. He was happy and contented. However, even this specially placid and contented child was destined to die one night at around eleven o'clock. He was just two years old.

It is a very hard blow for parents to have to surrender two such promising children to the grave within a few days, and then come to terms with their childlessness. Especially is this so for Wanja, who must now make the most of life as a blind person having been bereft of the joy and affection of his two boys. There is no way round it. It is hard, very hard.

Yet when I remember the look of sheer joy on Yasha's sweet little face as he saw heaven opened, I am very much comforted. I can still hear his cries of joy in my heart. I am expecting another child in April...

During those months neither letters nor parcels got through to Asia. Liesel's brothers and sisters back in Germany did what they could; but so often their efforts were in vain.

Wanja's recovery was painful and slow. He was frequently in despair, and it was as if he was drained of all confidence. Under these circumstances Liesel's firm, positive approach was an essential support for him. "The child I am expecting will need a cheerful mother, otherwise it will never be able to face the battles of life", she said to herself. Indeed, it was with similar words that she frequently sought to sustain Wanja when he was feeling down. But what a sorry figure the once brave Wanja now appeared; yet hundreds of thousands encountered the same fate.

In his advanced years, old father Thiessen took on the role of intermediary as far as sending on letters and parcels was concerned. At least in the European sector of Russia there was always some kind of postal service, even arriving from Siberia as well as Germany. Here is a letter which he wrote:

Dawlekanowo, 13th May 1932

"Let me not be put to shame, for I take refuge in thee." Psalm 25:20

Greetings in God's name, my dear nephew Heinrich and niece Friedl Muselmann!

Unfortunately the packets which you said you had sent have not arrived. I received four packets from my brother in Canada, and they took four months to arrive.

I shall be glad to undertake the forwarding of any letters and packets for Hans and Liesel. However, that is not without its problems. The regulations state that only boxes can be sent to Siberia, and I simply cannot get wood or nails here.

It is out of the question that Hans would ever be released from his exile. It may however be possible for us to get poor, dear Liesel to come here for a month or two. Yesterday I put in an application to that effect with the authorities. May God soften their hearts when they come to process it!

Captivity is particularly hard for women to endure. In addition, we have heard from Liesel that she had another child in April. They called him Eitelfritz. As with Liesel's other children, the delivery this time was also very difficult; but now she is overjoyed to have another child.

However, after just a week Liesel succumbed to the typhus fever which is rampant there. It seemed that no medication had the desired effect. In fact Hans was unable to raise the huge amount of money for the doctor quickly enough. To be sure, his eyesight has certainly improved, but he cannot undertake any demanding work, and of course as a result he cannot earn very much. We sent money straight away, but it never arrived.

On account of the infection, Liesel had to be admitted to hospital, and there they charge 20 roubles a day. Hans did not even have enough money to pay for Liesel's transport to the hospital. Eventually he found someone who would take her there against payment of some bread that he had. On that account Hans then had to go without food for several days. Liesel was so weak that she let the child drop out of her arms. She was dead weary. The little one died after six weeks.

It is truly a pathetic situation. As if their personal misfortune was not great enough, the officials there are so inefficient.

P.S. We heard yesterday that Liesel is off the critical list, and we thank God that she still has Hans. We still hold on to the hope that we might also see better times ahead.

P.P.S. The postman has just delivered one of the four parcels which you sent. The children will be delighted! I am afraid that my writing paper looks very poor. You simply cannot buy that sort of thing around here. We are reduced to searching out old account books so that we can tear out the pages which have just a few figures on them,

I wish you God's peace!

Jacob Thiessen

Meanwhile there was a development taking place in Germany, the dangerous implications of which went unnoticed by the majority, which would eventually impinge even on Liesel's own life. The event in question was the election of 1930 during which the National Socialists, under their leader Adolf Hitler, won as many as 107 seats in the German Reichstag (Parliament). Commenting on this outcome the noted author Thomas Mann had this to say:

"Let this election result be an admonition and a warning to us. Indeed, it should read as a danger signal of trouble ahead. No people can be expected arbitrarily to adopt the proposals which the National Socialists are in fact laying before the German nation, without our then becoming a danger to the whole world."

Only a few years later this prophecy became reality.

The situation in Russia had got the point where, for people living on both sides of the Ural Mountains, the issue was simply that of bare survival, and this was the tenor of Jacob Thiessen's next letter.

8th June 1932

"I will wait for the Lord, who is hiding his face from the house of Jacob, and I will hope in him." Isaiah 8:17

Greetings in God's name, my dear relatives whom I have not met and who live so far away from me! I have just received a letter from Liesel who informs me that she has she has received such a goodly sum of money from our children in Canada that she is able to afford the purchase of two pounds of flour. Naturally she is very happy. However, she does make a complaint about her swollen legs which are an outcome of the typhus she has had. The doctor who is treating her advises that she should eat more potatoes and pickled cabbage - a diet which would be pretty expensive. Both items are exorbitant, and it is ages since they had any potatoes. Liesel is having difficulty getting over the death of her little son.

The poor often have to move on somewhere else; and scarcely have they settled in when they are unceremoniously pushed on elsewhere once again.

Besides Liesel I also have two other daughters who are in similar straights. Both of their husbands have been arrested. Recently the youngest son faced a demand for 30 hundredweight of grain which he did not have. This was apparently a penalty for his not having taken any part in the production or harvesting of grain over the past years. It stands to reason that where, as in this young man's case, a person has to live on a hand to mouth basis, it is impossible for him to participate in the cultivation of grain for the community.

Who can say what the eventual outcome of all these things will be that are happening around us just now? It is now more than four months since I heard anything from my third daughter. I do not know what this means. If it was a case of death or some accident, either the authorities or relatives or members of the Mennonite church would let me know. As you can see, I am ill at ease and full of worries.

You ask about clothes. At the moment there are no clothes to buy here. It is not easy to find anything that might serve as underwear. However, under the circumstances at the moment we are sometimes obliged to do things which naturally go against the grain. Then again, one is also aware of the fact that there are considerable practical difficulties in sending things to us here, and in addition there is so much customs duty to be paid on any such items. On that account I scarcely dare to ask for.

Not long after that letter, there followed another highly informative message from the old father:

26th July 1932

"O Lord, to you I have committed my cause." (Jeremiah 11:20)

It is a special pleasure to answer your letters, particularly since all the parcels and letters you sent actually arrived, and the children have already received them. Believe me, it did them a world of good. Liesel asked me to confirm that she had received them. Just at present she does not have enough money for the stamps to put on an overseas letter, and should it not reach its destination, she would be very disappointed.

Liesel asked me to let you know that they are both in good health at the moment. She has written saying that, if God gives her sufficient strength and health, she would like to start working in the coal mine from 1st August, because this would bring in a bit more money. It is quite beyond me to understand how she can bring herself to work there as a woman. It is common knowledge that, even for healthy men, coalmining is tough, dirty work. I really hope that Liesel does not do herself an injury in the process, and I am concerned about her.

Here we expect the first decent harvest since ages, and it looks as if all the grain is ripening to perfection just on time.

I wish you all God's blessing and peace!

Your Jacob Thiessen

Half a year later, during 1933, the National Socialists seized power in Germany. The gulf between the peoples of Russia and Germany deepened, and so it was something of a miracle that Liesel's next letter to her brother Heinrich -written confirmation that she was still alive-arrived safely. It reached Germany via Jacob Thiessen, and this was to be her last surviving letter.

Anscherka, 16th December 1933

It is years since I heard anything from you. The line has gone dead. It could well be that you do not have my address on account of the fact that we have had to change house so often. I am sending you my new address with this letter.

My husband's stomach has suffered badly over the last years because of the poor diet and frequent starvation. Consequently I prepare meals for him as carefully as I can. However, when I bake bread without soda it is not light enough for him. There is nothing you can buy for baking here, not even yeast, and fresh dough is no use. Wanja is awake nearly the whole night, walking up and down, groaning in pain; and yet in the morning he has to set out for a heavy day's work in the mine.

In October I went digging potatoes in order to earn some money. It was just like we used to do it at home, and I felt so healthy and strong. Goodness, how can we ever hope to live again and make progress, with hopes of a better future, if we cannot get up and get on with it! Recently I was so full of confidence again, and we looked forward so much to the prospect of getting some potatoes, as they had definitely promised us. But they deceived us, as they did in previous years. We are simply not free agents here; and in spite of the hardest work, from early morning until late at night, we can scarcely feed ourselves. So where do you go to protest? We have been divested of all rights. We are prisoners.

This year the winter is very severe, and already the temperature has plummeted to 53 degrees of frost. At such temperatures the wind cuts like a knife. However, we do get some coal from the mine, so that we do not need to freeze when we are at home, and that is a lot to be thankful for.

In the meantime your parcels arrived, and once again they have saved our lives. The contents enabled us to eat to the full, something we have seldom been able to do over the last 15 years. We had almost got used to starvation....

It seemed as if an ever greater silence reigned over the vast tract of land in the east. The official interpretation of this "peacefulness" was that it symbolized the strength of the people; but in fact it was nothing other than a cover for the weakness of party and system.

Was it perhaps the silence of the graveyard? This was the thought that came to Liesel's brothers and sisters in Germany when they received no acknowledgement for any of the parcels or letters which they sent to her. It was therefore a special joy for them when, after two years, this letter arrived in Germany from Jacob Thiessen, indicating at least that he was still alive. It contained relatively good news as well...

Dawlekanowo, 6th February 1935

Things are looking up for Hans and Liesel. .. Hans has been transferred to another mine where he is better paid, and so his income is sufficient. At the same time I have my doubts as to whether the pair of them actually have enough to eat each day. For example, Hans could earn new income from the furs he has. Even when they purchase the cheapest items, they still only have 15 roubles left for the rest of the month. Because of this Liesel took on additional work in a shop in which vegetables were salted in barrels. However, it was too much for her.

Personally I have had much for which to give thanks and praise these past years, and since last year I have enjoyed such good health as I have not had for a long time. Moreover, I am well past 80 years of age! I am grateful every day for the blessing of good health, and I can undertake work today which in previous years I would not have contemplated. My sons-in-law have been released from prison. When the weather permits I visit my daughters turn about. If only Hans and Liesel could be here, my joy would be complete. I certainly would not be slow to visit Liesel, for she could make such wonderful pancakes. She just had a way of doing things, and her housekeeping was always such as pleased me.

I sincerely wish you all the very best, and please accept my hearty greetings. If this letter should reach you, please reply to it. May God keep us all in his grace,

Jacob Thiessen

In 1934 bread rationing in Siberia was brought to an end, and shortly thereafter Stalin's second five-year plan was put into effect. The Soviet Union also became a member of the United Nations. It was not possible on the basis of superficial knowledge to gauge anything of the terrible deeds that were being perpetrated by Stalin in the course of his notorious "purges" at this time. Well might father Thiessen have said then: "O mother Russia, history will certainly record you as one of its great martyrs whilst everyone round about you is shouting wildly: 'See, Comrades, how much better life is now; isn't life great!'"

So it happened that, after several years during which there had been no more news from their sister or from grandfather, the relatives in Germany assumed that the whole family had fallen victim to Stalin's awful purges. One day brother Heinrich made the decision to carefully gather up all existing letters. He put them in a large envelope and wrote on it:

"Elizabeth Thiessen, nee Muselmann, 1897-1935: the story of an orphan." Indeed, having stored the envelope in his attic after a gap of several more years, it occurred to him that these words were almost like an epitaph.

CHAPTER TWELVE

"MAMA, WE ARE ALL GOING, AND YOU REMAIN BEHIND ALONE."

House in Siberian Winter

"The whole dreadful truth about Stalin and his era has not yet been told. The worst part of it concerns the half-truths and the silences which are also lies."

Andrey Sacharov

"Things are looking up for them now!"

This remark of Jacob Thiessen certainly gives us occasion to pause and reflect on the fortunes of the young couple as they pursue their new career as exiles in Siberia. It was only after they had come to terms with the fact that there was no possibility of their returning to their old home that Hans and Liesel began to try and make something of their new surroundings.

"What cannot be changed must be accepted," they reasoned with one another.

Liesel had recovered surprisingly well, they both found work and thereby at least a modest income. They learned to fortify themselves against the lengthy and bitter winters in Siberia, even when this involved climbing onto the roof of their mud hut now and again in order to cover the chimney when the temperature dropped very low. However they were given coal from the mine in which they worked.

Hans and Liesel maintained a warm and protective love for one another which helped to lighten the drudgery of their daily work routine with many shafts of humour and happiness. To be sure Wanja lapsed every now and then into despair concerning the hopelessness of his situation, but Liesel always knew how to cheer him up again, and she had a knack of being able to cheer him up just when he needed it.

Siberia itself experienced a gradual development in its infrastructure. A street would be completed in one locality, and bit by bit the cities themselves appeared to grow bigger. Perhaps nowhere else did Stalin's drive towards the expansion of his Russian empire show itself so strongly as just here in Siberia, a land rich in mineral deposits.

Liesel had something special to remember about the summer of 1937. At long last Wanja was able to fulfil a pressing desire, namely, to complete a lovely wooden house. They were glad to see the end of their time in a mud hut, and the couple moved into it even before they had installed windows, doors or the floorboards. To be sure, relative to German standards, their "dacha" was plain. Nonetheless, it held out the promise of being a real home for them, and the wood breathed a wonderful scent of resin and fresh pine.

Liesel celebrated her 40th birthday on a stifling hot day in midsummer that seemed endlessly long, and was also teeming with midges. She had something very special to celebrate on that day because, in spite of being up in years, she was again expecting another child. The young couple took this as a hopeful sign of new beginnings for them after all the many trials and tribulations they had been through.

Meanwhile, hidden behind the walls of the Kremlin, Stalin shrouded himself in an air of mystery as he secretly plotted further purges and show trials. In that regard, the year 1937 has come to be known as the "black year" in Russian history. Occasionally, as she was hoeing and weeding in her long, narrow strip of garden behind the house, Liesel had premonitions during those long summer evenings of what lay ahead.

These thoughts would almost seem to outweigh the joyful anticipation she had concerning the child that would be born. Wanja sensed that his wife was anxious about these things, and he sought to divert her mind from them. "Look", he suggested, "anyone in your condition is bound to have some worries," as he tried to make light of Liesel's forebodings. Nonetheless, behind a cheerful facade, Wanja himself was becoming increasingly uneasy as he heard the news of more and more arrests, none of which was in the least justified.

As autumn drew on the days became shorter. Those Siberian nights! How dark they could be when there was scarcely a star to light up the sky. As people began disappearing from their place of work each morning one by one, all sorts of rumours were whispered behind upraised hands concerning the terrible circumstances under which this or that person had been seized during the night. Wanja quietly stowed away a satchel for carrying food and warm clothing in the event that they might have to take flight.

Then one November night -Liesel was in the sixth month of her pregnancy- the military police broke into their house, which still lacked locks on the doors and which was incomplete in other ways. They shouted, "Get out, Wanja Thiessen!"

Wanja quickly grabbed his provisions and clothing from where he had hidden them, and suddenly he was surrounded by the police. "There is no need to handcuff me," he retorted firmly. Wanja then turned to take leave of his wife: "Make sure to bring up our child as well as you can!" This was as much as he could blurt out as he bade Liesel farewell. For a moment he gazed at her with a look that was both deeply affectionate and serious. Before she knew it Wanja had disappeared into the Siberian night accompanied by his captors. As Liesel reflected on that parting, it took her a long time to take in the full significance of what her husband was communicating to her.

Every evening when she returned from her work, she would eagerly search for the first glimpse of her house from a distance to see if there was even a flicker of light in the windows, for this would indicate to her that Wanja had come back home. However, every day all that she saw was darkness. Christmas came and went. Then it was time for her delivery; but still there was no sign of her husband; a deathly hush enveloped the house.

Once again Liesel experienced great pain in the delivery of this her last child, and it was necessary to call the doctor. Fortunately there were adequate medical provisions to ensure a safe delivery. It was a strapping young lady doctor who attended Liesel at the birth. She listened sympathetically as Liesel told her something of her story. Then, as her birth pangs gave the young doctor cause for concern, she asked her: "It seems as if it is going to be a matter of life and death once more, so who do you wish me to save, the mother or the child?"

"We should save the mother," Liesel replied, "because the child will die without her in any case. Perhaps we shall both be taken from this life ..."

Miraculously both survived, and a little boy was born to Liesel on 18th February 1938. Out of the overwhelming sense of relief and thanks that she experienced immediately after the delivery, Liesel momentarily forgot her anxieties about Wanja. She named the child John-Heinrich in memory of her eldest brother.

The neighbours all lent her a hand on the way to full recovery. Liesel still retained hopes even then that Wanja might return. She nearly wore herself out as she made her way, carrying her child, from one office to another with an official petition to the authorities. No one was heartless enough to simply laugh at her, so they merely shrugged their shoulders when she made enquiries. Slowly, painfully it dawned on her -an awareness that she had really suppressed all along- that Wanja would never come back again.

"Why? Why?" was all that Liesel could ask her German and Russian neighbours day after day. But her companions could only say, "There is no point in asking the question 'Why?'" A number of them about that time relapsed into a stupor of apathy. They became as indifferent to their daily work as they were about their untidy appearance, and they allowed others to push them around. Drunkenness was the habitual state of the few men who were still there. Whenever they appeared their eyes had the same sad expression which could be seen on the faces of the shaggy pit horses that pulled the carriages.

Liesel herself made every effort to ensure that she did not slide down the same slope into despair. She completed the house, knitted for the little one and developed the garden as far as it was possible. As soon as three months after the birth she was ordered back to work, although no longer in the mine. She realized the situation in which she was now placed. The breadwinner was no longer there, and so her only recourse was work. Liesel was a hard worker, and there was no shortage of work in Siberia. Shortly afterwards she was allocated a post in which she could take her baby with her. As soon as she had weaned her child, he was taken into the crèche which was normal practice. In accordance with the strategy to realize Stalin's work plans, every available hand was needed; and the workforce got lectures about that every day.

"I will not leave you orphaned, Elizabeth Thiessen." In the long winter evenings which followed, the lonely mother often turned to these words in her heart. She clung fast to the thought that her young son would now be her comfort for the rest of her days, nor did she wish to be ungrateful for such a hope.

Little John-Heinrich was a contented boy who was easy to bring up. He was already able to stand on his feet when he fell seriously ill on a bitterly cold winter's day. Dysentery was again making its rounds amongst the children in the crèche. Liesel really thought at one point that she would never see the end of his ailment as she had to nurse him night after night, carrying her little crying child up and down in the living room. She felt as if she had never been so distraught in all her life. Surely God would not allow her misery to continue in this way.

Yet Liesel had an exact instinct for the inevitable. Even this, her fifth child, she was going to have to bury. It was on 12th February 1939, just before his first birthday, that he closed he eyes for good. "Mother, we shall all go, and you remain behind alone!" It was precocious little Yasha who had once uttered these words to his mother. If Liesel recollected these words once during the day, she remembered them a hundred times. In a sense Yasha had "broadcast" his own death, after which Liesel had had this remarkable premonition concerning the other children, even although she was only aware of its fulfilment subsequently. Of course she did not want it to be reality for the reason that she had the deepest fears about being left all on her own in this huge land.

Liesel was so exhausted from weeping and caring that she scarcely noticed how supportive her neighbours were to her in her hour of need. They thoughtfully ensured that the grave for her little child was appropriately dug and prepared for his burial. Even in the midst of all the atheism in Siberia, it was heartening for her to hear them speak words of blessing and hope for the future over his coffin.

Now there was no one left who belonged to her. Or perhaps there was. Far off beyond the Ural Mountains her aged father-in-law was still alive. Liesel was aware at that moment of his tender thoughts reaching out to her. It was truly painful for her now to have to inform the old man about the death of his youngest grandchild so soon after his own son had been abducted. She wrote briefly and to the point. Perhaps she was no longer capable of feeling; or maybe she feared that reproach, anger and despair would get the better of her. Naturally her father-in-law would be hurt if she were to write in those terms.

" ... There is no point in destroying ourselves through bitterness," the old man had replied. His shaky handwriting betrayed the trouble it took him to put his thoughts down. "Let your soul possess itself in peace before God; for he will help you, and you will experience his provision for you. 'Those who sow in tears will reap with joy'. Do not throw away your confidence, and support others around you who are also bound up with you in miserable circumstances."

"It is hard to live without companionship," Liesel was to confess later when she spoke of this particular phase in her life. As she recounted her trials, her voice quavered even after many, many years had elapsed.

Jacob Thiessen advised Liesel that she should make a specific effort to seek out company to relieve her loneliness. Her needs were largely met through the small Mennonite-Baptist group which had formed and which used to meet secretly in houses for fellowship. At the same time, Liesel pluckily sought companionship with her workmates, and she even took up writing letters to Germany once more; but she never got any reply. Not one of her letters ever reached their destination. Eventually she came to understand that "home" is a word which has a largely spiritual connotation. She realized that "home" gains real content more by what we ourselves contribute to it, than by what we take out of it.

A year after what for Liesel was a particularly traumatic time in her life, war broke out again in Germany. Hitler had concluded a non-aggression pact with Russia. As a matter of fact people in Siberia were not really aware of what was going on in the rest of the world. News items from outside Stalin's empire were deliberately excluded so as to keep the population in the dark. Daily life followed its usual course: a pitiless routine of gratuitous violence, forced labour and harsh commands. Time and again there were severe economic setbacks.

Meanwhile Liesel had started work in the brick factory. It was gruelling work, but the pay was not bad, and it was a bonus to have cheerful work companions. Then, with the onset of Spring, when the light on the horizon assumed new colours as the days lengthened, Liesel's indomitable will to live reasserted its authority over her feeling that the Lord had deserted her. Summer was just round the corner, and she eagerly anticipated working again in the little patch of garden which had come to mean so much to her. Of the few items of news that did get through, Liesel learned of Hitler's breath-taking victory over Poland. This aroused her hopes. She fancied that a victorious Hitler would certainly open up the way for all Germans in Russia to come home! She would be able to get back home again to the land of her birth. Thereafter all those terrible years in Siberia would disappear from her consciousness like a protracted and frightening dream.

"ALL YOU NEED TO DO IS SIGH"

German POWs, Stalingrad

"O what are we human beings?
A dwelling place visited by gruesome agonies!
An orb filled with deceptive happiness,
Short-lived flashes of sunlight!
The scene of stabbing fears
That sharpen sorrow's pain,
Snow that rapidly melts away
And a burned out candle..."

Andreas Gryphius

In reality there was little time or energy left over for this lonely woman in Siberia to expend on idle thoughts during the day. This was a mercy in itself, for it helped her to come to terms with her situation. But then March 5th, 1940 arrived, a day which would radically alter her whole life for years to come.

As was her practice every day, Liesel set out for her work in the brick factory on this morning early in spring. It was still bitterly cold, but already the midday sun had begun to project brief glimpses of bluish light on the glistening snow. The day's work was nearly done, and twilight had appeared. The final wagon of bricks was almost full thereby fulfilling the required tally for the day. Just a few more bricks were needed, but these were the very ones which could not be found anywhere. There was not a single brick that had been fired which could be found throughout the entire factory. However, there were a number of bricks to be found in a ditch which was not more than a few metres from the factory. The problem about getting them out was that, on either side of this ditch a great pile of loose, broken bricks had been heaped which were only kept from collapsing on account of the severe frost that welded them together. A handful of the required bricks lay between this great pile of broken ones in the ditch; but the least movement would cause the whole lot to come crashing down. The overseer was in a hurry to finish to get off home.

"On with the work! Pick up those bricks over there!" he shouted, pointing to the ditch. However, not one of the women moved. They all knew it would be suicidal. Livid with rage, the brigadier bellowed: "Thiessen! You fetch them! You don't have a family! And if you refuse, you will be deprived of three months wages and food!" There was no doubting that in the interim these commanders of work brigades had themselves become little Stalins.

The harassed woman set out on her mission with the utmost caution. She carefully moved forward, putting one foot gingerly in front of the other. Oh if only she might avoid the temptation to wish to stop at the wall of bricks! The other women held their breath as they watched Liesel pick her way deeper and deeper into the ditch. Liesel bent forward in order to gently loosen one or two bricks and then attempt to lift them clear.

"Forward march! We must get finished!" yelled the brigadier impulsively. Just at that moment Liesel turned round - and then it happened. The left hand wall of bricks collapsed and, as it did so, the tremors caused the right hand wall to follow suit. Elizabeth Thiessen was buried alive under a pile of bricks. Just before she lost consciousness she said to herself: "This is certainly the end - and it is not so bad."

When she regained consciousness again there were at least ten men busy trying to dig her out so that they could lay her on a stretcher.

"My right foot is missing! Please take my foot with you!" she groaned, pleading in despair. One of the men sought to pacify her: "Your foot is still on, hanging by the flesh!" Thereafter Liesel lost consciousness completely.

After the event, she could not recollect accurately just how long she had lain unconscious. She came to herself, once more wide awake and lying on a board, to find herself smothered in a thousand bandages. She gathered that she was in hospital. Later she found out that she had been taken to Anschero-Sudschenk. To begin with she tried opening her eyes as well as listening to the sounds around her, but she failed to register the slightest sensation from the outside world, either through her eyes or her ears. It was only after a marked period of time, the exact length of which she could not compute, that her various senses slowly recovered their normal powers. At the same time, she would repeatedly relapse into unconsciousness so that she did not know where she was.

The first definite thought of which she was capable concerned her aged father-in-law. Surely it would only be right that he, of all people, who had always helped her to shoulder her troubles, should be told of her present plight. But who would write to him? At length it happened that a German woman who was coincidentally in the hospital said she would be glad to write a few lines to Jacob Thiessen. It was only with some difficulty that Liesel managed to remember his address. In the letter that she dictated she said that she had been buried alive. She was constantly in a state of unconsciousness because of the pain she was suffering, and she could not pray any more - not ever.

"My dear child, I pray for you day and night", Jacob Thiessen wrote back. "Just concern yourself with breathing! It is sufficient if you just sigh!"

The doctors who looked after her in hospital were very good, and in addition a good number of them were exiles. Liesel once remarked jokingly, "Perhaps Dr. Zhivago was among them!". From time to time this severely injured patient had the impression that people were actually waiting for her to die. However, as the state of her health made miraculous progress over the months, it occurred to a young couple who were doctors that they might show Liesel the X-Rays which had been made of her injuries when she was first admitted.

"Your pelvis was completely crushed," stated the couple with justifiable pride at their achievement. "Your back was broken in three places, but without any paraplegia. Four ribs in front as well as the collar bone were also broken. And what about that foot? Would it ever regain normal usage?" Once Liesel had looked at these photos and had understood their implications, she fainted again. It was well over a year before the patient could stand and make any progress in walking with the help of crutches. As the doctors saw her passing, their appreciation of Liesel was unstinting: "She's got real guts," they remarked.

News of what was happening in the world outside came to Liesel more readily in the hospital, even although what she heard was only in dribs and drabs. It was on a hot summer's day in mid-summer when Liesel was already able to walk outside with the aid of crutches, that one of the other patients told her that Hitler had surprised Stalin with a sudden attack on Russia. The man added: "Of course that will certainly mean that the war will spread to the Soviet Union. You watch; Hitler will get his fingers burned!"

Indeed, it was on the very day when, long ago, Napoleon himself had mounted his campaign against Russia, that Adolf Hitler announced the start of his war against Russia on 22nd June 1941. "Stalin is sure to liquidate all the Germans living here," was the rumour which quickly circulated round the hospital. Liesel shook her head in disagreement. "That will not happen in Siberia," she commented, "because he needs us to provide the workforce for his ammunition supplies." Apart from which she herself had long ago become a Russian citizen by virtue of her marriage to Wanja.

After she was discharged from hospital, Liesel was classified by the doctors as unfit for work; but the system was merciless towards her. Once again she was exiled and assigned to a work unit. However, with the help of detailed medical reports, she was given a lighter post as an employee in a State run sewing company. She already knew that she would not receive her pension for another fifteen years. Life in Siberia for those who were exiled consisted in nothing but work. This soulless activity was often characterized by wasted efforts or pointless inactivity, enforced by harsh regulations.

Liesel was keen to work, but to begin with the effort involved in getting started again was painful. Her back was in constant pain, and she could only walk with trouble. To be sure, there was a time when, in obedience to the maxims of Marxist-Leninist doctrine, one was encouraged to promote the rights of the working classes at every level of society. In the meantime, however, the masses had effectively been stripped of their rights, and it was only an élite that were beneficiaries of the new system. There was only one hope remaining now, and this was that the German troops would be victorious. Liesel wondered if her elderly step-father had been caught up in the initial stages of the conflict between the German and Russian troops. Subsequently she was unable to pinpoint the exact date of his death, but she knew that some of his family were in America, some in Germany, and the rest were in Russia. They were thus all placed on mutually opposing sides. He might well have pictured the world as a pathetic madhouse.

It would appear that some of Liesel's German cousins took part in the assault on Russia, for their deaths are recorded as taking place there at this time. As she worked away at her sewing table in the workshop, news filtered through that the Allied forces had sent help to the Russians by supplying them with arms. Then, over the course of the war years, a considerable number of German prisoners of war would turn up in her neighbourhood. The drawback was that any communication with them at all invited the death sentence, and so she gained no information about Hitler's rapid advance. Notwithstanding, the name "Stalingrad" began later on to be picked up in conversations by those who were keen of hearing. The only problem was that there was no way of telling whether the appalling details of that battle were in fact true or not.

The war became very drawn out, and whilst food rations were reduced, work allocations were sharply increased for those who were fit enough to work. Many were compelled to work in the ammunition factories, and there were certainly times when Liesel had cause to be thankful that she had been buried alive, for it meant that she would never have to go back into a factory. As she perceived that everyone around her was taken up with the basic fight for survival, Liesel not only fed herself by what she was able to grow in her plot, but she also shared that produce with her neighbours, thereby enabling them overcome the worst of the hunger. Even potatoes grew during the war years, and they were not stolen, for there was a tight system of security in Siberia. Besides which, there grew up a close-knit community amongst those who were exiles which actually ensured that there would be no underhand dealings of that sort. "Many a time," Liesel was to tell later, "I would cut a potato or an onion in half so that we would all have something."

On her 47th birthday, 20th July 1944, Liesel went to work as usual. On that lovely mild evening she was very happy as she anticipated the arrival of some neighbours. Although there was not much in the way of food with which to celebrate, yet the main thing was the convivial spirit they shared with each other. It was only decades later that she came to learn how fateful a day this had been in Germany's history. The tragic events which had overwhelmed her homeland put an ever greater distance between Liesel and her own people. In fact she still had a deep sense of homesickness; but now she would have difficulty in identifying exactly where she was homesick for. Moreover, coming to terms with all the grief she had experienced was not the work of a day. In the first place there was obviously Wanja, whose return home she no longer expected; and who can gauge the reluctance with which a human heart will acknowledge that a loved one who is missing is dead? Then she missed terribly the sweetness and liveliness of her children, not to mention her warm hearted step-sisters and her courageous step-father.

At long last, after many years, peace was restored again, or at least a state of affairs prevailed that went by the name of peace. There was great rejoicing throughout Russia over Stalin's victory: Churchill and Roosevelt had aligned themselves with him. Now the furthest reaches of Stalin's domain actually came to within a couple of dozen kilometres of Liesel's birthplace, the estate at Schweinfurt. Stalin's photo was posted high up on every building in Russian cities. To be sure, Russia had suffered much, yet the sacrifice had been worth it.

But what of German victims who had fallen throughout the length and breadth of Russia, besides those who had died in European countries, as well as in East Prussia, Pomerania and Silesia? Those who lose in a war must keep their counsel. There could be no doubt that Russia, that great empire of states which had triumphed with the aid of the Allies, and Germany, a small country that had been crushed, would each face a new year in 1945 with completely different perspectives. Hitler's whole enterprise had ensured that there was not a whisper of sympathy for the defeated people of Germany. Of course, Stalin was no better; but then he had won.

Franklin Roosevelt, the American President, was not spared to see the end of the war as he died just before Germany's capitulation. It is just possible that he might have been able to bring about a workable peace treaty in Europe. It was through his help that Russia had defeated Germany. Nonetheless, in no time at all, two great power blocs were shortly confronting one another as military opponents; and that was a tragic twist at the end of the Second World War.

In the early part of the post-war era Russia found herself increasingly isolated by the nations of Western Europe. Liesel had not even heard of the persecution of the Jews during her time in Siberia. Thus it transpired that, in the course of these post-war years she adopted more and more characteristics of her adopted homeland. There was a peculiarly Russian quality about Liesel's attitude to a number of things: her fatalism, her capacity to endure suffering and her childlike faith. She also manifested a complete indifference towards all that went on in the world at large and anything that did not immediately affect her own life.

Meanwhile Germany itself was harshly divided by means of a concrete wall and barbed wire. So it came about that the soldiers of the Communist regime pursued their sadistic vigil from lookout towers by day and night in order to shoot the fugitives.

CHAPTER FOURTEEN

NEW HOPE

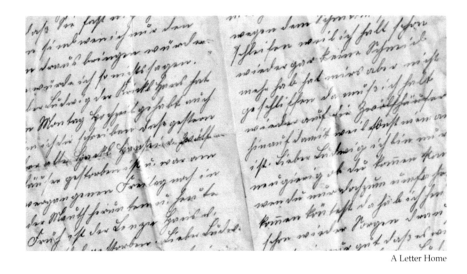

A Letter Home

Double the watch over this grave,
So that Stalin may be kept in it forever,
Along with everything that must pass away.

J. Jewutschenko (Russian poet)

Liesel's story in Siberia continues as we find her living out her life as a member of a collective-style group. On account of the fact that she was now entirely on her own, she needed this kind of communal existence, and indeed she adjusted to it very well. There followed a succession of peaceful years, unpunctuated by any dramatic events, in which she was able to carry out her daily work unhindered. Liesel's new pattern of life was quite unaffected by such occurrences as the bombing of Hiroshima, or even Stalin's bold claim to the city of Berlin. Admittedly, if the 'buran' winds should shake her little house during the depth of winter, she did sometimes vividly recollect memories of her past life, such as playing the piano at home and later in the house of her parents-in-law. Music and books, songs and pictures. These things now all belonged to a far off world. She had lost any desire to make the most of her life. Liesel said herself, "From this time onwards I will close my heart to anything new." Yet that is easier said than done; for each of us is stirred from time to time by some striving after a greater awareness of reality.

One morning in March 1953 a neighbour of Liesel's, Anna Ewert, knocked at the door of her house before daybreak. "I have some news for you," she whispered secretly, "let me in." She slipped quickly through the door. "The old man Stalin is dead."

"What news you bring! And was it a natural death?" Anna became even more withdrawn. In those quarters the awareness had grown in recent times that there were eyes and ears spying in every quarter with a view to distorting everything to suit their prejudices.

"How should I know that?" she continued. "The story goes that he had arranged beforehand that all his personal physicians should be murdered. Did one of them perhaps have the courage to turn the tables on him? As usual, we shall never know. But the main thing is, he is dead!"

"You know that for certain?" said Liesel. "Thank God! Things could not get worse, so now they will start to get better! Who knows, I might even start getting letters from Germany again! Who is going to succeed Stalin?"

"I do not know, you old optimist," replied Anna. "His heirs may start to fight amongst themselves, and we could wind up with another phase of anarchy."

"That's the last thing we want, Anna," suggested Liesel. "The civil war was even worse than the years of the Stalin era. It was then that we had our worst experiences."

The entire workforce had to participate in the solemnities surrounding Stalin's burial in the Kremlin which were broadcast on the radio. With expressionless faces and tight lips they intoned the national anthem in a mechanical fashion:

"O flag of the Soviets, wave O standard of the peoples,
Lead us from victory to victory...
Be true to the nation, as Stalin taught us... "

In fact there was no outbreak of anarchy after Stalin's death; but the Kremlin did witness several occasions of disharmony. It was the execution of State Secretary Beira at the end of 1953 that finally saw the beginning of the so called process of "de-Stalinization".

It was really from this time onwards that Liesel had a longing, which grew stronger every day, to finally learn something about her relatives in Germany. The older she grew, the more vividly did her own childhood come back to her; and so naturally she wanted to know just how her brothers and sisters had come through the terrible years of the war. Day succeeded day, months and years went by without her hearing anything from Germany. As Liesel had lived in Anscherka since 1931, it never occurred to her that none of her relatives in Germany would not know her address. For their part, her family were completely in the dark about her own whereabouts, nor did they make any enquiries.

No doubt due to the long periods of unconsciousness which she had experienced after her serious accident, Liesel had completely forgotten all the addresses of her family in Germany. Now she wracked her tired brain from morning to night trying to recollect them. Eventually she was able to retrieve part of the address of her Aunt Frida. It was impossible that that quiet, faithful relative of hers would have forgotten Liesel.

The letter that Liesel wrote to her Aunt Frida did not have the complete address on it, and so it took some time before it reached its destination. However, Liesel had not heard the news that her Aunt had died over twelve years ago; that her uncle Benjamin had married again; and that he himself lay terminally ill in Mannheim General Hospital where his eldest daughter was in charge as hospital matron. However, Uncle Benjamin, who was a Professor of Theology, was well enough known for the letter to find him without any great difficulty. When he received this sign that Liesel was still alive, he was already nearing his own end and so could not register his surprise as strongly as he would have wished. After his death, his wife diligently wrote to all those who had conveyed their condolences. But in what terms was she to reply to this confused letter, obviously written by the shaky hand of an old person, which had come all the way from Siberia?

Uncle Benjamin had maintained contact with many Germans who were exiled in, or had emigrated to Russia. Indeed, most of his energies had been expended in trying to assist them. Many of them had communicated to him their sincere thanks for all that he had done for them. Was it possible then that Frau Thiessen was simply one more grateful correspondent? Clearly she was related to Uncle Benjamin's first wife. Nevertheless, in this large family, with all its many connections, she simply did not know where to begin. Moreover, what could she possibly know of the brothers and sisters involved in this request; and how could she tell that this woman so far away in Siberia was desperate for news of her own people? In the event, she sent back a reply which stated in formal terms that her uncle had indeed been glad to hear from her, but that there was really no point in continuing the correspondence.

Have we any idea what "waiting" means? As she waited for news from Germany, Liesel had to confess that she remained a beginner in the art of patience.

At long last Liesel eventually received an answer from Uncle Benjamin's second wife whom she did not know. There was no mention of brothers, sisters or other relatives. Was that all? Was it conceivable that her own family no longer wanted to know anything about her?

The painful silence continued on through summer and winter. Then the 62 year old woman finally received her hard-earned and well deserved pension. Many a night she lay awake and tried to puzzle out the meaning of this complete break in communication on the part of her German relatives. Otherwise Liesel was little aware of the other events that were taking place around her.

Meantime Khrushchev had taken over the running of the Soviet Union. The "sputnik" proved to be a considerable technical achievement, and it circled the earth for a short while. Indeed, it was a Soviet citizen, Alexander Gagarin who was the first to set out on a manned space flight around the world. Russia's development as a major power in world politics was so swift that other countries in the non-communist bloc became alarmed. After the crisis of the Berlin blockade in 1948, it was the Cuba crisis of 1962 which brought the world once again to the brink of nuclear conflict. During those decades the West scarcely got any real insight into what was happening internally inside the U.S.S.R. Boris Pasternak wrote his novel, "Dr. Zhivago", which was banned in his homeland. Meanwhile, thousands of people continued to be exiled as political dissidents to the remote corners of Siberia. Elizabeth Thiessen was numbered among them. Indeed, it was only now that she really became aware in her old age of the extent to which she had lived in hope of being able to return to Germany once again to see her brothers and sisters.

"Elizabeth Thiessen, I will not leave you forlorn..." Now her dear father-in-law Jacob was no longer around to sustain her. "Make use of the support which you have to hand," he had once advised her. "Don't let go of the rope whilst you are hanging over the precipice!"

"Oh, no!" Liesel said to herself, "God has not kept his promise!" She was simply overwhelmed by bitterness, anger and despair in her loneliness. So her neighbours were right after all: there is no God! What folly to place your confidence in a figment of your imagination! Plainly Liesel was past the age when she might better weather these storms of disappointment.

Liesel was now confined to bed, and soon afterwards she suffered a complete nervous breakdown. At night, when she was affected with asthma, her breathing became difficult. She became so weak that she could not even make herself a cup of tea or boil an egg. It appeared as if her mental faculties had seized up, thereby preventing her from remembering anything or anyone. She seemed to lose the will to live; she passed her days in a gloomy, confused state. If anyone called to see if she needed any help, she almost scolded them. It was the first time in her life that she had thrown in the sponge like this.

At the same time, she was far from being abandoned. The German women who were her neighbours showed exemplary care for her as they patiently waited on her various needs, fed her, ensured that her house and garden were kept in order, and provided her with basic necessities. They also summoned medical help when needed. However, this state of virtual paralysis lasted more than several years.

Anna Ewert proved to be a particularly devoted neighbour who would often stay with her overnight if required. Anna had a shrewd insight into exactly what it was that was making Liesel so homesick. As soon as she could sit up in bed properly, Anna repeatedly asked her: "Try to remember, if you can, Aunt Thiessen, any part of the address of your eldest brother. Did he not live in Bavaria? And if he is no longer alive, he will certainly have relatives." Sadly, Liesel's befuddled mind just could not function properly.

During the following winter, Liesel was able to take more initiative in looking after herself, but she did not leave her house. Her front door was detachable in the middle, and whenever her friends knocked at the door, having brought her milk, or soup or boiled potatoes, she would open the upper section of it and take it inside.

Slowly, almost imperceptibly over the next months Liesel recovered her composure and, more important for her outlook on life, her faith in God revived once more. Then one spring evening during 1966 the miracle happened. Suddenly the veil that had hung over her memory was drawn back, and she was able to remember a section of her brother Heinrich's address. For Anna, this fragment was all she needed. To be sure, the postal exchanges generally between the West and the Soviet Union had not become all that better since Leonid Brezhnev had succeeded Khrushchev in 1964. At the same time, Anna knew from experience that letters from Siberia would certainly reach their destination in East Germany. She herself had relatives there with whom she was often in correspondence. Now all that was needed was an opportune moment to persuade Aunt Thiessen that she should write to her brother. Fortunately this too proved possible.

So it happened that one day Jacob Riediger's family, who lived in Bohringen über Mittweida, near Karl-Marx city in East Germany, received a letter from their niece Anna Ewert in Siberia:

"...My dear Aunt, I have a special request to ask of you. There is an elderly lady living here, Frau Thiessen, who was born in Germany. She has lost all her relatives. I feel really sorry for this old mother, who has had to bury all of her five children. Her husband's name was Hans Thiessen, and he came from Schonau in the Ukraine. I have helped her to compose the enclosed letter in order to help her find her near relatives. Could you please arrange for the radio or T.V. to put out a request for information? This would be a great favour for the old lady. She came to Russia as a teenage girl when she was fifteen. Although she herself is in poor health, she has always been generous towards those who are poor and sick.

My daughter gladly assists her in her home, and she has often received kindnesses from Frau Thiessen. If she is out of water, my daughter goes to fetch it for her. I collect her mail from the Post Office, and also do her shopping at the grocers. Sometimes I take bread and soup to her, for during the winter months she is sorely troubled with asthma, and she does not go out of doors.

When you get any news please write to my address. Aunt Thiessen's address is the same as mine, except she stays at block 68. I have enclosed part of the address of Aunt Thiessen's brother, as well as the short letter she has written."

Immediately on receipt of this letter Jakob Riediger wrote to Heinrich Muselmann, someone who was unknown to him, and whose address was incomplete. He also enclosed Liesel's brief message.

As he then posted this inadequately addressed letter that same evening, he chuckled to himself: 'What a strange turn of events! Let's trust the ever reliable German Post Office to find the addressee.'

AT LONG LAST, A SIGN OF LIFE

Passau

How undramatic are all true miracles

Antoine de St. Exupery

The sun shone brilliantly on that May morning in 1966 as the dawn rays highlighted the three rivers which flowed through the historical city of Passau. The surrounding countryside in the south of Bavaria was bathed in the warmth of a golden morning. There was a contented atmosphere about the forecourt of the estate at Pfarrkirchen as the light flooded the landscape. Just then the estate manager, Heinrich Muselmann, was returning from his first visit through the estate and the cowsheds. This glorious morning made him very happy. In a few days he would be celebrating his 70th birthday. It would be a joyous occasion in which his children and family would take part. As his son had taken over the running of the estate from him some time previously, this relieved him of many of his worries.

He already had five grandchildren, and the arrival of the sixth was expected that summer. Although he had early on in his marriage been left a widower, he was nonetheless grateful for the many kindly providences which had marked his life, the beginning of which had not been at all easy for him.

He went to his office to look through the letters that had arrived. Among them he saw that there was a letter which had been sent from East Germany. Turning it over, he did not recognize the person who had sent it, and he noticed that the writing was plain and unsophisticated. The address was incomplete, but the letter had still reached him. He opened the envelope and read the following message :

Mittweida, 2nd May 1966

Dear Sir, The enclosed letter from Frau Liesel Thiessen has been sent to me from the Soviet Union with a request to assist in the search for her relatives. It may be that the church offices could help in giving information concerning the whereabouts of the person mentioned.

Jakob Riediger

The significance of this letter did not immediately register with Heinrich, but then his heart began to beat faster. He was certain that this was Liesel's handwriting, but it was clearly also that of an elderly person, shakier and interspersed with Cyrillic letters in some of the words. "Good gracious!" he muttered to himself; but before he had finished reading to the end of the letter he had called his wife. Together they bent over the letter and read the following:

Anscherka, 19.3.1966

My dear brothers Heinrich, David, Rudolf, and sisters Anna and Martha! Greetings in God's name!

It was back in 1932, dear Heinrich, that I last heard from you. I seem to have lost you all, yet long so much to know which of you is still alive. Can you tell me which of the uncles and cousins is living? Is there anyone who can inform me what the situation is?

I have now spent 54 years here in Russia, and for the last 35 years I have been living in Siberia at Anscherka. If it is God's will, I hope I

116

may discover what has happened to you all.

With my warm greetings from your sister, niece and cousin.

Liesel Thiessen (nee Muselmann)

The couple gazed at one another in astonishment. Someone whom they had assumed was dead was actually alive. Even the most original novelist could not have invented something as strange as this. In the silence between them they both realized that this letter would change their lives. It was Heinrich who spoke first: "If possible we will bring her back here. Then after all the pain of her trials and isolation she will at least have a nice home with us." There was a lengthy pause and then he continued: "Of course, it could well be that she would not be the easiest person to put up. She will certainly be in poor shape and will need nursing care. I remember how determined she was as a youngster - just like myself."

His wife nodded in agreement, adding with a serious expression: "I believe we could cope with her - don't you think so? It would certainly be a labour of love to give a person with that kind of story a home."

The news about the apparent "resurrection" of their sister Liesel, whom everybody had assumed was dead, spread like wildfire amongst her relatives throughout the length and breadth of Germany. Apart from two of her brothers, Christian and David, the rest of her brothers and sisters were all alive. Even most of her uncles were still living, but nearly all her aunts had died. To be honest, we cousins really did not know what to make of this name that everyone was now talking about. True, my mother had once told me as a child something of the tragic life that Liesel had experienced; but at that age her account seemed to me to belong to the realm of fantasy. However, when he heard the news about Liesel, my father, Liesel's uncle Hans, was very moved.

Of the many letters which from this time onwards winged their way beyond the Ural Mountains, not one has survived. Nonetheless, we do still have Liesel's first reply. It is clear that several factors had a hand in what she wrote, not least her emotional excitement, lapses of memory and her age. The letter itself is several pages long, and here are some of the things she said:

Anscherka, 25th May 1966

My very dear and precious brothers and sisters.

You may be separated from me by a great distance, but you are very close to my heart! "God does great things which we cannot comprehend." (Job 37:5) Amazing to hear from you after 32 years! And even more so to know that, with the exception of Christian and David, you are all alive! I honestly did not expect to receive any more letters from you ... I simply assumed that you were not alive, or that you did not want to have anything more to do with me. That made me very sad, and I wept a lot to think that that might be the case ... I learned to commit everything to God.

From 1962-65 I suffered a mental breakdown, and during that time I forgot everything and could undertake no work. I had to ask my neighbours to help me with the simplest tasks... I cried to God that he would give me an understanding heart to accept your silence. It was a dreadful experience. Then, one night, whilst I was dreaming I remembered part of Heinrich's address ... When your letter eventually came I was so overjoyed at hearing from you that I was sick for three days, so that I could not immediately write back to you ...

Thank God, I am in as good a state of health as can be expected for an elderly person of my age. I live in my own little house which my dear Hans built for me in 1936-37. It was as if he knew what lay ahead and was saying: 'My dear Liesel, this is for your old age.' In 1937 he just disappeared without a trace. After his departure, little John-Heinrich was born and lived for a year. Then he too went to join his other three brothers and his sister in heaven. Thus I am left childless and widowed. It is just as my little Yasha once said: 'Mama, we are all dying, and you are here alone.' I lost count of the number of times that he said things like that to me!

Every month I collect my pension which I have earned by hard labour. That provides me with sufficient on which to live a frugal existence, and I am happy with that. Meantime, I have learned that not a hair falls from our heads without God's permission.

I have been ill a number of times. I have twice had typhoid, once facial erysipelas ...and once appendicitis. I had a serious accident in which my back was broken in three places, as well as fractures in my hand, foot and collar bone. Thereafter I was afflicted with a severe bout of asthma, and I constantly felt drained of energy. I have brought five children into the world only to have to bury all of them. I have had tuberculosis of the foot. On five occasions we have had to start from scratch to build our lives again, and we have moved house 25 times. My motto is: "Love your destiny, because it is God's way of reaching your heart ..."

Please give my greetings to all the rest of the family. I shall try to write to them all. I can sadly no longer remember Rudi, the youngest, as my memory is failing me now. As I think of each of you quietly in my heart, I silently give to each a hug and a kiss, for I am so overjoyed that we are once again in touch with one another. Your long-lost sister and sister-in-law,

Liesel

In a flurry of activity, there were many parcels which were sent off simultaneously from these homes to the sister they did not realize they still had. Her brother Heinrich explored the possibilities of Liesel being able emigrate. He received a reply from Moscow that in such circumstances it would only be the next of kin who would be allowed to leave, i.e. mother, son, father, daughter... This prompted my father, Hans Hege, to send a petition to the German Embassy in Moscow which was largely successful.

Liesel herself could speak Russian fluently and she could also read the language very competently, but she could not write it. However, this would have been necessary for the completion of the many petition forms which were now being sent on her behalf. To this end she would need a scribe who was also able to phrase matters in a skilful manner. Even so, the Russian militia at that time were just as adroit at finding ways of turning her down.

Liesel wrote of her feelings at this time:

Goodness knows how much hassle all this form-filling will involve before I attain my object. May God reward you all for the great efforts you are making on my behalf; and may they not end in being to no effect. You ask what I would like for Christmas. Frankly, my dearest wish is simply to be reunited with you!

In the light of her journey home Liesel was eventually advised to contact the Russian Red Cross, because they would be able to arrange for her to be transferred to the German Red Cross. She wrote:

Anscerka, September 1966

Dear brothers and sisters!

...For the first time in my life I have had to water my cabbage in September on account of the exceptionally good, dry weather, such as would have been thought impossible for this area at this time of year. Who knows, it may be the last time I will do this ... Tomorrow I shall go to the local militia headquarters in order to see to the petition. Without permission from Moscow it is impossible to do anything around here...

I am sending you a photo of me, from which you will see that I have become somewhat smaller. The reason is that my back is bent, and since the accident I also have a hunchback. My routine here has been one of unremitting hard work. However, my dark hair is genuine, not tinted! Thank you for your photos. Do you know, I will need time to get used to how you look, for I still remember you when you were all young! It is wonderful that at your ages you all look so fit and carry your years so well!

The beautiful summer days we enjoy here are over for another year. In this region, from the end of June to the middle of August, it only gets dark very late on in the day, whilst dawn comes very early. Now darkness descends much earlier, and it is pitch black and so silent outside ..."

With the onset of autumn, Liesel gathered in the produce of her garden. It was the finest harvest they had experienced since she went to Siberia, and she wrote extensively about it in her letter. Would this also be her last harvest in Siberia? As she gently turned over the soil in her little plot, the realization deepened that, in and through all that she had seen over these past years, this was truly her home. With a sigh she recollected the enthusiasm with which she had prepared the ground each year. The toil of endless summers seemed to be rewarded in this last, most glorious summer. And did the rain ever water that dear soil so tenderly as the many tears she had shed over it; or the hoe furrow the earth as sharply as the sorrows which pained her heart whilst she worked there? Without knowing it, her life in this land of Russia had been deeply influenced by the love of Russians for their land.

"No form of patriotism, no matter how zealous, can match such an attachment," her father-in -law had once told her many years beforehand. It was only when the awareness dawned on her that she was actually leaving Russia that the truth of that statement became clear.

In order to help them ripen, she took the dried out tomato plants and hung them on a string from a shelf in the kitchen. In that sort of weather they never ripened well outside. Siberia! When she was a child, the name had sent shudders of fear through her whole being. Now, lost in thought, her mind ranged over those many winters that she had survived in Siberia as an adult. How could she forget the music of the icicles clanging in the winter frost, or the uncanny silences, or the beauty of winter landscapes that seemed almost unreal, or the graves of her five little ones. Suddenly the conviction gripped her: "You will leave much of your heart behind you in this land."

"You look a completely different person!" With a look of amazement, this was how Liesel's neighbours greeted her. "Of course, those lovely food parcels and all the good news from Germany has made all the difference"

During the following winter Liesel gave careful thought to the question of whom she should sell her house to in the event of her leaving Anscherka. Ah well, it was true what she now felt, namely, that in spite of all the joy of looking forward to her journey, it was in fact no easy thing to break camp and set out on an unknown future with just a suitcase. Here is what she wrote in December, 1966:

The daughter of a lady here, Frau Ewert, who is a doctor, went to the chief of police to enquire on my behalf about a visa. They told her that they had never had to deal with anything as unusual as that, nor would they know how to process it..

In spite of this setback I still hope to be able to come home to you. I have learned over these past weeks that "nothing is impossible to God". All your letters express a genuine warmth of love as brothers and sisters such as I have longed for my whole life. I thank God that I keep happy and that I am able to think more clearly. Even my asthma is improving. As I get better it is really a joy to anticipate seeing you once more...

When New Year came, Liesel gave a party in her little house. She took delight in describing all the details about the lovely scented parcels she had received, and how the rooms in her house had been decked out with the many sparkling decorations sent to her from West Germany, the gold and silver stars, gongs and tinsel. The whole community in Anscherka took uninhibited pleasure in this happy turn in Aunt Thiessen's fortunes. At the same time, she herself looked forward with composure to her 70th birthday. Mind you, she said that she would really believe that she was on her way home only when she had alighted from the train in Germany.

Then in April her emigration papers actually arrived at the military authorities in Anscherka. "Sometimes I am afraid that I will die before I can leave," she wrote. In fact just before she was due to depart she had a bad attack of fever which laid her low. However, her desire to see her family again was stronger than all the hardships she encountered.

Anscherka, 6th May 1967

Dear brothers and sisters! ... This will be my last greeting to you from Siberia. If God allows, I hope to leave here tomorrow at 9 o'clock in the evening, and I shall be travelling alone to Moscow. I shall arrive there on the 10th May. As long as there are no problems -you never know what may happen- I will take a train that night straight to Berlin.

Long before the trans-Siberian express arrived that evening, a huge crowd of well-wishers from the whole community at Anscherka had assembled, as if on a pilgrimage, on the station platform. They all wanted to be there when Aunt Thiessen started out on her homeward journey. Russians, Tartars, Germans and native residents of Siberia all jostled one another to have a share in bidding their dear adopted aunt farewell. As the train was only scheduled to have a two minute stop at Anscherka, the good natured Russian conductor was somewhat alarmed that the tearful partings between Liesel and the host of sorrowing babushkas seemed to go on for ever. However, as there was no one from the military police to interrupt the proceedings, the train driver only drew away from the station when the crowd had had a chance to settle down a bit. "I shall easily make up the few lost minutes here on the long stretch ahead because this is such a good time of year", he said, chuckling to himself. "It was on account of my being so small," Liesel recounted afterwards with pride, "that the trans-Siberian express was held up."

On through the night the regular clickety-clack of the wheels on the rails suddenly reminded Liesel of the journey she had made as a young girl when she had travelled from the Ukraine into all the uncertainty of internment. That experience now lay more than fifty years in the past. As the night wore on, many varied images from those decades presented themselves to her wandering mind. It seemed as if her whole life came under review; and if it had not been for the pain which she constantly had from her broken back, she might well have concluded that it was all just a bad dream. Then the first grey streaks of dawn appeared in the sky. The rose tints of early morning silhouetted the Ural Mountains in the background against the sky as they passed Sverdlovsk. Siberia lay far behind her.

Now the train was approaching the outskirts of Moscow with its many towers glistening in the sunlight. The faces of those whom Liesel could see seemed somehow friendlier, and they appeared to be dressed in a smarter style than she had seen in Siberia. The old men looked just like Tolstoy himself. "There you are," Liesel thought to herself, "although I have been in Russia for so long, I have never visited Moscow. What an amazing land this is..."

When she arrived in the capital, Liesel began to experience something of the endless treadmill of officialdom which plagues every visitor.

To begin with they would not accept that Liesel was German. Everything about her convinced the customs Officers that she was a genuine woman from Siberia. However, although all her papers were in order, they wanted to retain her as an interpreter. What saved her was the fact that she had never learned to write Russian. Eventually one of her interrogators came up with the suggestion that she must have money since she had sold her house in Siberia. Of course that was correct, and so she was forced to leave behind all the money she had, and so state who should be the beneficiary. "You are not allowed to take one rouble over the border with you," declared the inspector. At this point, when Liesel was close to losing her patience, she jokingly said to them, "Come now, my friends, is this the way you treat an old babushka?"

Later that evening the train travelled on in the direction of the West. Along the way they passed the stations in places where well-known battles had been fought. How much had the peoples of both races suffered who in a mysterious way were united in Liesel's heart.

As the train made its way through the night towards the Federal Republic of Germany, a deaconess in Holland on the other side of Europe also set out in order to meet the homecoming invalid. This was Liesel's younger sister Martha who worked there in the Deaconess centre at Amerongen. A year ago she had been very ill herself, and during that time she had often had vivid dreams about her sister in Russia whom she missed so much. When her condition was at its worst it had been the cry of her heart that God would at least give her some token of reassurance concerning her sister's existence, whether she was dead or alive. Just a few days later Liesel's first letter had arrived. Martha had saved up her whole holiday entitlement for that year in order to be able to spend the time with her sister. Although it was not normal practice for deaconesses to be allowed to take their holiday outwith their appointed rest home, an exception in her case was gladly agreed to.

Although they were many kilometres apart, both women sighed as they waited patiently for the endless border-crossing formalities in the East German sector to be concluded. Even Liesel's· toothpaste tube was squeezed! "Look, my dear, you should try and respect my humanity, and not just carry out regulations," said Liesel to the woman official who was undressing her. It was only when she had shown the receipt certifying the amount of roubles that she had left behind that she was allowed to proceed. On the evening of 11th May, 1967, shortly before Whitsun, Elizabeth Thiessen stepped onto German soil once again after an absence of 55 years.

Martha was already waiting on the platform as the train pulled into the station. The joyful anticipation of seeing her sister again had made her appearance much younger, so that Liesel only recognized her because of the dress she was wearing. The two sisters, who had separated as children, fell tearfully into each other's arms. As a formality every returning citizen had to register at the transition camp in Friedland. Martha had already notified the authorities prior to their travelling onwards. The border official had listened sympathetically to her story, and then he said "No one will be processed here at Friedland during Whitsun. You are welcome to go to your home meantime with your sister." "Home," for the present meant staying with Jacob. He had even kept the telegram intimating Liesel's arrival in Passau.

During the journey Liesel took in the countryside around her with utmost interest. "Oh how lovely everything is here in spite of the devastation caused by the war," she remarked with amazement after they had left East Germany. "All these lovely new houses! But how small a country West Germany is! Here we are already in Bavaria! Was Hitler not aware of that? Otherwise he could not have started a world war."

On their arrival they saw that they would have to contend with an army of journalists and reporters. Liesel's sensational homecoming was all the talk in Germany. To begin with she did not understand a word, as she was unfamiliar with the Bavarian idiom. However, she never lost her composure. Everything would soon fall into place.

As she crossed the threshold of her brother's house, the family struck up some verses from Psalm 138 as a means of welcoming her home: "I praise you, O Lord, with all my heart... because you have kept your promise. You heard my prayer when I cried to you. The Lord is mighty. Nevertheless, he has regard for the lowly and undertakes for them... Although I may pass through sore trials, you preserve my life..."

In that moment it was as if all her inner tensions found release. First the beautiful posy of welcoming flowers slipped from the clenched hands of this small, slight woman. Then, overwhelmed with gladness, she swayed slightly before falling into the arms of her sister Martha. She cried her heart out. The long pent-up miseries of so many heartaches found relief in her sobbing. Liesel's homecoming was like that of a wandering child who finally returns after many an arduous adventure.

A STRANGER IN THE WEST

Hohebuch

"There may well be lovelier times in life, but this is our highpoint."

Jean Paul Sartre

"At her brother's country home," wrote a reporter for a newspaper in southern Bavaria, "Elizabeth Thiessen is now able to enjoy a peaceful retirement after many years of great hardship. Doubtless she often dreamed of just such a home during the decades she spent in Russia." But goodness, what a strange thing is the human heart!

During the Whitsun holidays all the brothers and sisters arrived at Jacob's home. Thereafter Liesel had to make the trip to Friedland to fulfil her immigration requirements. This too went without any mishap, and she was able to satisfy all 16 of the different officials as to her bona fides. Indeed, they proved to be friendly and helpful. Back at Jacob's house no trouble was spared to make Liesel feel at home. Martha went shopping for clothes with her sister, and assisted her with her washing. She also arranged for Liesel to be seen by a doctor, and she took time to listen to her many stories. It was not always easy to follow the thread in Liesel's recollections, partly because she could not yet express herself adequately in German, and partly because her memory failed her at certain points. The family showed great sensitivity in respecting the limits of her health, as well as the fact that her digestive system could not cope with every sort of food. In particular, they were conscious of the hard life that she had had.

For all that, Martha was deeply concerned about her newly returned sister. As she herself went back to Holland at the end of her holidays, the one thought which preoccupied her was the question as to whether Liesel would be able to make the necessary adjustment in her new circumstances.

Such fears were not without foundation. For quite some time Liesel was not nearly as happy and contented as she had anticipated she would be. Everything was so strange! She had left Germany before the First World War, and now there was nothing left to remind her of what had once been there. To be sure, the Deutschhof was still much as it had been, and her brother Rudi had taken her there soon after her return. But what else remained? She could remember almost nothing about the First World War, she was just as ignorant about the Third Reich and she knew even less about the Second World War. What an immense change had come over the German peoples during these years! But what of herself? Had she not meanwhile become more of a Russian than a German? Liesel remembered a statement of Dostoyevsky's that Uncle Benjamin had been used to quoting in earlier years when he could not make sense of the Western world: "They have a different soul." Admittedly Dostoyevsky had spoken these words about the Americans; but were they not now equally applicable to the whole of the Western world? Was this at root the reason why she found life here in Germany so enormously stressful? Thus when she went into a bustling store crammed with all sorts of goods and asked what a night-gown was like, she would be shown pictures of twenty different models. Then again, she was not used to making independent decisions, for the Soviet model of society ruled out altogether any possibility of free choice in regard to life-style.

Whenever Liesel wanted to cross the street she had to stand in the midst of what was literally a breath-taking procession of cars, and wait for the light to turn green whilst she inhaled their petrol fumes. The crowds rushed around the city in their bright, trendy summer clothes, seemingly bent on meeting hectic deadlines. Their faces were drawn and anxious as they raced past each other. No one seemed in the least aware that we are all members of the same human race. Everyone apparently knew so many people, but few had any time for real personal encounters. These strange people seemed to be identified more closely with the film-stars, about whom Liesel knew nothing.

Every day she was confronted by a flood of special offers, prospectuses, advertisements, price reductions, information and newspapers spilling through the letter box. The whole incentive was to buy, buy and buy! The T.V. projected its own stream of gaudy images into the living room, and the radio blared out music round the clock. Liesel noticed that the people here were so well provided with life's essentials that they spent much of their time in needless diversions and superficial activities.

Also there seemed to be a continuous round of street parties, company outings, holidays and special trips being organized. She asked herself if the men and women amongst whom she now lived ever gave any time to the consideration of how to live and die? In fact she was so bombarded by numerous different impressions that she was no longer able to take in anything new in a meaningful way. She found that she had forgotten it the next day. Nothing made a deep impact on her any more. Market forces locked those in independent employment into a pitiless fight for survival. The very process by which they had come to possess all that they wanted had driven them into a spiritual alienation which they were scarcely aware of. To the newly returned immigrant it appeared as if her German compatriots would suffocate in their consumer-oriented world.

In this situation it was not surprising that Liesel struggled every day with new and perplexing questions. In addition, those early weeks of her return to Germany marked the start of the "youth revolution" in the 1960s. She found it intolerable that these spoilt young people should set stores on fire and go about fighting in the streets. In her eyes they were devoid of idealism and they rejected any form of authority. She had no real grasp of the disturbing events which were then taking place, events which were to end in a way quite opposite to that which was intended. Liesel expressed the forthright view that "The West is a sink of corruption!"

When she lay awake at night her mind went back to the broad stretch of night sky above her in Siberia, with its clear, sparkling starlight. She thought of the deep quiet of her former surroundings, broken at most by the occasional barking of a dog. She forgot about the daily grind to eke out a living, nor did she remember the bitter cold or the unyielding pressures to conform. Instead she called to mind her former neighbours, modest, simple people with whom she felt far more in sympathy than with her brothers and sisters whom she had grown away from, and whose speech, interests, cares and problems she hardly understood.

"I am a stranger in this world!" was the firm conviction which she came to about her circumstances. In her new setting she noticed how people required some kind of "framework" within which to establish their human identity: a house, an estate, a car, money, a respectable profession, or an academic background; and if you were a woman, you needed to enjoy youthful good looks and be elegant. But Liesel had no such "framework". Moreover, whenever she met people who had any official capacity, or clerks who worked in stores, she sensed that they treated her as a second-class citizen on account of her strange accent. Of course this wounded her pride and dignity; but whenever she tried to protect herself from such mistreatment, the attempt invariably failed. People just laughed at her and did not take her seriously.

In this connexion I was given much food for thought when I came across a heavily underlined letter which Liesel had preserved. It had been sent to her from East Germany where some Siberian friends of hers had gone to visit their children in Thüringen. They had succeeded in making a visit to relatives in West Germany.

Here is what they write to Liesel:

> *"We are glad that we have returned here to East Germany. We could not endure all the pomp and pride! You have everything you want over there - a beautiful house with all imaginable comforts, and so much good food. But goodness, look at what you throw away! We felt as if we were poor relatives by comparison. Such a luxurious lifestyle is very demeaning to us: you should be ashamed! If you were at least humble and thankful enough that life had not treated you as harshly as it has us ..."*

There was no doubt that it was also hard for Liesel to find herself in the role of poor relative. To be sure, her brother Heinrich immediately set about arranging her pension, and in this respect the prisoner of war postcard from the First World War which he had kept played a decisive role. Yet part of the problem lay in the fact that such an unusual case as Liesel's had never arisen before in West Germany, so that it took a little while before her money became available. In the meantime, she was forced, in the absence of any other wherewithal, to beg for each stamp and for permission to make every 'phone call. Many a time she had the impression that it would have been easier for her brothers and sisters if she had never returned.

"It is a shame," wrote the Russian authoress Tatanya Goritschewa, "that the West has not learned the value of suffering."

Liesel took trouble to settle in as well as she could, there is no doubt about that! When she could get her thoughts straight, the first thing she tackled was the relearning of the German language, as she considered this her first priority. However, the German language had changed considerably during the 55 years that Liesel had spent in Russia. It is touching to read the comments and notes which she made in the process of relearning her native tongue, for they reflect a significant aspect of German cultural history since the Second World War. Her notebook contains such words as jeans, pullunder, T-shirt, job, hobby, stress, happy-end, team and other loan words. Liesel had learned the meaning of persistence during her life. On one page of her notebook she wrote this thought: "You simply must show them that you are determined to live." Immediately following those words she then added a Russian proverb: "The person who becomes a sheep will be eaten by the wolf." Finally, the more familiar she became with her surroundings, the less did she feel it necessary to hide her opinions from others. Thus she was convinced that her estimate of the corrupt West was 100% correct.

Her brothers and sisters were astonished to discover the extent to which Liesel's whole outlook had been conditioned by Soviet ideology. For decades she had heard nothing good about this hated Western world. In addition it must be said that the lack of a complete formal education deprived her of the capacity to form an objective viewpoint. For example, differences of opinion with others in the family would arise from time to time simply because Liesel did not understand what they were saying. Whenever such conflicts arose, Liesel's old tendency to state bluntly what she felt reasserted itself. In this regard her brother Heinrich's temperament was not at all unlike her own. But would things work out positively in the long run?

It was therefore a bitter blow for Liesel that, after just a year in her homeland, her sister Martha died suddenly after a short illness. Martha stood closest to Liesel in disposition and affection, and the two sisters had arranged to spend their retirement together. Liesel was devastated. When she recovered somewhat, she simply said, "God makes no mistakes. This is what I have learned, and we must compose ourselves accordingly." However, this did not make the situation in her brother's house any easier.

After two years Heinrich took his courage in both hands and wrote to his uncle Fritz who was in charge of Mennonite homes for elderly people throughout West Germany:

Gatehouse, 7th February 1969

Dear Uncle Fritz!

Liesel is capable of settling in, and yet she seems not to be able to … All of us here have really put ourselves out in trying to help her. She was welcomed with open arms. Each time there were real difficulties in the house, we simply put the issue aside and tried time and again to make a new start. Liesel did not understand us. Then again we have tried to keep in mind the fact that for decades on end she has been subjected to nothing but Soviet propaganda. Inevitably that has a formative influence on a person, even when they themselves are unaware of it.

We regret that it is no longer possible to entertain Liesel any further. To begin with we simply let matters ride, but then we gently introduced the idea that, in due time, the best solution for her might be a good retirement home. At this Liesel threw a fit and was ill. Seeing that she had regained sufficient health by the beginning of November last year, the doctor suggested that the carpets be changed. In fact this was more with a view to helping my wife, who is now at the end of her tether.

Could you please let us know what it might cost to stay in one of your old people's homes? Thereafter we will be able to decide what is right … Until that time we shall probably send Liesel on one or two trips … With best wishes,

Your nephew Heinrich

What Liesel has written about that year in which she was "shuttled" between her brothers and sisters, as well as other relatives or convalescent homes (in Karlsruhe or Franconia), is full of deep self-reproach as well as criticism of others. Her whole being seemed to alternate between indignation and disappointment. The phase through which she passed gives no evidence of self-insight. Indeed, she seems to despair of herself. On the few occasions when she mentions homesickness for Russia, her recollections are seen through rose-tinted spectacles and do not reflect reality.

She recovered her health remarkably well, and she was able to celebrate her 72nd birthday cheerfully and in good spirits. The event was, however, completely overshadowed by Neil Armstrong's moon landing which took place on the same day. Liesel did not begrudge the Americans in the least this triumph which had allowed them to plant their flag on mother moon. It was ten years previously that the Russians had obtained the first interesting photos of the far side of the moon through their space venture Lunik. The photos appeared in all the Russian newspapers. Was that not much more progressive? "Now the two superpowers are fighting over the good old moon - how childish!" Liesel stated.

By this time she had become aware of the fact that, in the West, a person could say what they thought without being sent straight into exile. At the same time, it must be stated that she actually made very little use of her right to free speech; but when she did, it was impossible to let some of her statements go unchallenged if we were to take her seriously. Sadly, as she grew defensive, it was not always easy to reach an amicable conclusion with Liesel if you were having a conversation with her.

Another striking fact to emerge was that, in her lively and frequent correspondence with Uncle Hans Hege, there is not the slightest hint on Liesel's part of any tension in the family. This would indicate that she was aware that she had not always spoken or acted correctly. Liesel knew that Uncle Hans would have got to the root of any problems she might have mentioned.

What was the solution to this problem? Surely there must be some permanent place which, in the course of time, would be appropriate for our returned Aunt. Liesel for her part decisively rejected any thought of going into the care of an old people's home.

"That would just suit you!" she blurted out in a forthright manner. "In Russia one would never send a relative to an old people's home! Did I come back to you only to be shoved into a home?" Behind these vehement words lay a good deal of the tenacity and passion that had long characterized Liesel. Clearly she identified an old people's home in Germany with an alms-house in Russia.

Every one of us in the family circle put on our thinking caps in order to find a way forward. On the one hand, some members of the family were still so caught up in their daily work and business as to have little time to spare for the needs of an extra person who was occasionally unwell. On the other hand, others were themselves elderly and therefore not in a fit state to care for someone else. In some situations the accommodation in the house was not suitable; and in other households there were small children whose demands kept parents fully occupied. The enquiries we made among ourselves did not frankly reflect well on us as a family. We had no room for someone who was homeless! There was a time, during the war, when no sacrifice was too costly. However, we had now grown accustomed to our comfortable life-style, and this inhibited us from setting aside our selfish priorities. We were dependent on innumerable people and things. We had forgotten how to love.

Writing to a relative, my father, Liesel's uncle Hans suggested what seemed to him a practical option:

Hohebuch, 28th June 1969

…Liesel is unhappy. She is homesick for Russia. I had no idea there were difficulties.

We have given consideration to the possibility of how we could manage if she came here to Hohebuch. She had spent some time here. However, aside from the fact that I myself am 84 years old, and could well need looking after, there is the fact that in the hectic round of activities here she would probably feel that she was not needed. Nobody would have time for her, and she herself would not be of much use to anybody. In all likelihood she would be very unhappy. I have therefore thought of another plan.

Liesel went to school in Heilbronn. That whole area right up to Breitenau is familiar to her, and would indeed be like a bit of her former home territory.

*Moreover there is a warm Mennonite fellowship there, and she really stands
in need of such company. Then there is the fact that she has a sister-in-law
in Heilbronn, Gertrud, who is the widow of her brother Christian who died
some time ago. In the light of this I have acquired a newly built house in
Heilbronn for both women. It has three lovely sunny rooms, and will soon be
ready to occupy. The two step sisters happily anticipate being able to move
into this nice new home. In the meantime Liesel is sharing accommodation
with Gertrud in her step-sister's present house.*

How sadly my father deceived himself! The two women were not at
all happy to be sharing a house. For one thing they were like chalk and
cheese together, and for another they had lived on their own for decades.
They had each mapped out their own definite routine which inevitably
clashed once they were put together. Gertrud had become extremely
independent and, on account of Liesel's ignorance of how people in the
West live, there were plenty of ructions between the two of them in the
confined space of that house!

Although Liesel said nothing more to anyone - and she certainly was
submissive to the commanding presence of her Uncle Hans - yet she felt
lonelier than ever. In the meantime, however, she had learned trust, and
she held firmly to the promise once given her so long ago: "Elizabeth
Thiessen, I will not leave you forlorn." The door which now opened was
completely different from any human expectation.

Liesel and her sister-in-law stayed in the attic flat of a house in which
the ground floor was occupied by Herr and Frau Birnbaum who were
landlords of the property. They had an elderly mother who still lived with
them. During the day the couple were both fully taken up with their work
and of course they were absent. It then happened that the elderly mother
required occasional attention. At least it was no longer possible to leave her
on her own the whole day. So Liesel offered her services to the couple in
what was for them a difficult situation, and she undertook to care for the
basic needs of the old lady and generally to look after her. Liesel had a real
heart for people who were elderly, sick or suffering in any way, and this
was certainly a sphere in which she was confident. In addition, she was still
strong enough to be able to undertake a certain amount of physical work
relating to these tasks. As Liesel set herself to this new responsibility with
zest and good humour, the old lady herself improved markedly. Thus it was
that the one who had appeared so inept in her new surroundings suddenly

found that she was fulfilling a role to which she was temperamentally and even physically suited. In addition, it gave her a real sense of fulfilment. Liesel faithfully attended to this old lady right up to the end.

As a mark of gratitude the couple left her all the old lady's furniture. Of course this meant a great deal to Liesel. From having possessed nothing, she now at least had some furniture and belongings which helped to foster the sense of "home" once more; for she had truly won the old lady's affection. Meanwhile, the time for Liesel to move in with Gertrud was drawing nearer. Eventually it was her sister-in-law who wrote to Uncle Hans stating quite openly that she could not entertain the prospect of living together with Liesel. Here is an excerpt from a letter written by Hans Hege to the Birnbaum family:

Hohebuch, 17th August 1970

At the last moment Frau Gertrud Muselmann has indicated that the two women do not get on together.

From the outset I could of course have sought a two room house for my niece. Needless to say this would, under the initial agreement, have made her really lonely and unhappy, because she was always used to living in a community where she had neighbours.

In the meantime my niece has had the opportunity of looking after your late mother. She is overwhelmed at the generous manner in which you have recompensed her services. Furthermore, now that she has the possibility of accommodation in the attic of your house, including all your mother's furniture, she will feel somewhat at home. One can say that she is now beginning to put down tentatively the first roots in her new environment.

It is the cause of considerable humiliation for us all that there is not a single member of the entire family who has been able to offer her the security of a home such as you have just done. On account of her many trials, I would kindly urge you to continue showing this lady, who is the daughter of my eldest sister, the same esteem as you have demonstrated to date.

Frau Gertrud Muselmann intends moving into the new accommodation on her own. Would you please ensure that the sum due for Frau Thiessen's rental is charged to my account...

Liesel was happy to continue in the cordial atmosphere of the Birnbaum's home. She soon recovered her accustomed zest for life, one token of which was the constant round of visits she made, and the many people she never tired of entertaining. Liesel even looked altogether a much younger person, and she was still able to make ends meet with her pension. Indeed, she gave the impression of having made a definite effort to put the past, and all its trials, behind her. Liesel clearly intended to open up a new chapter in her life in which she would enjoy to the full the fresh possibilities which now offered themselves to her. Sometimes she reminded me of a child that was content to live for the moment at hand. In addition, the local Mennonite fellowship in Heilbronn gave this much travelled woman a warm welcome.

Once when I visited her she confided, "Since I returned to Germany I have learned more about the East and West than I ever did during the course of 30 years. I sometimes feel as if I am going to be torn in two. What can I do to reconcile these two conflicting sides of my experience?"

I replied by mentioning the saying of Gracian (1602-1658): "One half of the world laughs at the other, but they are all fools!"

For a moment Liesel looked serious, and then she said: "Yes, perhaps they are fools; but laugh? No, my dear, that is the last thing we did in Russia. Moreover, I don't laugh here either. Just living with each other causes us all a lot of anxiety. Life has taught me to look terror in the eye, and that transforms anxiety. From time to time I ask myself whether all of us - in the East as well as in the West - have not suppressed what we ought to have seen and recognized. Had we the courage to assess things as we ought to, that in itself might assist us in overcoming to some extent the fears which we entertain about others and also about the future."

During the course of the following months Liesel received visits from all her brothers and sisters.

"In the midst of the various endeavours undertaken by all of you, it is vital to draw a firm line under whatever may have gone wrong. At least you have been able to share some pleasant days together," my father wrote. "And dear Liesel, please, please try to accept that we are all acting with the best of intentions and entirely in your best interests. The wounds of the past will heal; but do not allow them to fester by continually giving way to

The fact is, and this needs to be recorded as well at this point, that Liesel was no paper saint; she was a human being with all the contradictions that that implies. Thus whilst on some occasions she seemed to us to be quite contented, there were other days when she was the picture of fury. This is what one has to bear in mind. In Siberia misery was the common lot, because everyone had either had a relative who had been abducted or who had been murdered. There was a desperate need for each other. On the other hand, there was no danger that envy would rob a person of their inner peace. Yet here was a completely different situation confronting Liesel. She saw how her brothers and sisters enjoyed undisturbed security within the warm circle of family, children and grand-children.

The realities of hunger, poverty, cold and pain were light years away from their experience. Under these circumstances, the path to freedom and a thankful heart would best come by pressing ahead unflinchingly with the task assigned to one. In the course of time she won through to a victory in these lessons of experience as well.

Once when I had 'phoned her to find out how she was getting on, she replied: "At the moment I am doing just fine. However, it seems that, as a general rule, things are so ordered that I don't get on so well. Let's just see what happens next!"

"Does that mean," I replied, "that you do not expect any more good out of life?"

"Well in fact," she said, "it is just that I have never experienced periods of tranquillity for any length of time throughout my life. I just assume that this has been necessary for me. Without the winepress there is no wine."

Shortly after this conversation she had a stroke, and she was admitted to the hospital in Heilbronn. However, it was only a mild stroke, and she was soon able to return to her beloved home. The second stroke, which followed soon after the first one, was of a more serious nature. It was during the time when she started to take exercise again, walking along the long, spotless corridors, that she realized that she could no longer look after herself. So what was to happen next? Liesel was a proud character. She wanted to be able to be independent and free. It was nothing short of a nightmare for her contemplate the possibility of going into an old people's home. It was wise in the first instance not even to mention the subject. In any case, she needed time in order to reach her own perspective on this new turn of events.

"Oh dear," she sighed, "what else will still be demanded of me?

Was this God's will for her? Then there would be no avoiding it, and it would be pointless to struggle against it.

"Please do whatever you think is right," she said to my father one day. He had gone to a great deal of trouble in seeking a solution to her future. "Everything will work out well. At long last I have stopped worrying about myself."

CHAPTER SEVENTEEN

HOME AT LAST

He Is Risen!

"An old woman crosses the street. She has brought up a family, and has received nothing but ingratitude in return. She has worked hard and now lives in poverty. She has loved and now she is left alone. However, she is far from bitter, and she lends a hand when she can. A neighbour, watching her go her way, declares: "One day a brighter future will dawn for her".

Victor Hugo

Uncle Hans Hege wrote in these terms to the Birnbaum family, in whose house Liesel continued to have right of dwelling:

"We have been in touch with a well-appointed home for elderly people which incorporates care facilities. Frau Thiessen will soon be released from hospital. We have received a promise that there will be a place for her in the hotel within eight to ten weeks. I wanted to let you know about that now because by that time her apartment in your house will be free. As soon as it is convenient for you, I would be glad to discuss all matters relating to her rent...

It is with sorrow that we contemplate Frau Thiessen's departure from the flat in which she was so happy, and from the people amongst whom she had found a new home. However, she recognizes the necessity of this solution, and she is quite agreeable to going into the old people's home..."

"It has been a set pattern of my life that I have had to move from one place to another until I reach my destination." As she comforted herself with this statement, Liesel suddenly chuckled with merriment.

After she had been released from hospital, she was taken by some Mennonite friends to recover at the castle farm in Lautenbach which was only a few kilometres away from Heilbronn. Liesel spent the weeks there, during which she was waiting to get into the home, with the tenants, a married couple Ernst and Lise Landes, who were themselves not young. In fact the son had already taken over responsibility for running the establishment, and the other members of their family lived for the most part away from the area. Frau Landes was a motherly figure, in spite of which it was a considerable strain on her to care for someone who stood in need of her warmth and kindliness. At the same time, such was her nature that she could do no other.

"I feel really at home here," Liesel said sometimes. It was meant thankfully, yet there was also suppressed sadness in her voice as she looked out from her comfortable little apartment onto the lovely expansive fields surrounding Lautenbach castle farm. There is little doubt that, in such an atmosphere of indulgent patience and attentive care, Liesel felt a sense of security such as she had scarcely ever enjoyed in her life before. Indeed, the whole surroundings in which she now found herself would remind her daily of the happy childhood she had spent at the Deutschhof.

In fact it took longer for the· spare room at the home to become free than had been planned, but as far as Liesel was concerned she was quite at ease with that. Visitors all had the impression that she was by now fully integrated as a member of the Landes family.

Liesel was later to describe the next development as a kind of miracle. Herr and Frau Landes decided to keep Liesel with them permanently. They had no illusions about the task they had taken on. Nonetheless, they saw plainly that this was what had been given them to do.

"It is remarkable just how things turn out sometimes in life!" This was Liesel's comment to us. "In fact," she continued, "when once you have inwardly surrendered about a specific issue in being willing to carry it through, one is released from the burden."

My father was delighted at this new turn of events, and he shared his pleasure with us when he gave us the good news. He was never at ease with the prospect of allowing Liesel to go into an old people's home. In his letter he summed up his feelings on the matter by saying: "It is literally a wonderful solution. This is Christianity in action. "

Many a time, Liesel thought to herself, I imagine that I am in some delightful garden in Paradise. Such were her thoughts as she sat of an afternoon in summer enjoying the balmy weather in the garden below her apartment. It was a sort of alpine garden, slightly set apart from the castle, in which there were many quiet corners. The scent of roses hung in the air. Everything about it breathed goodwill and pleasantness.

Aunt Liesel Thiessen had by now become part of the furniture amidst the wider circle of the Landes family; and even when her own children were present, Frau Landes never lost sight of Liesel. She learnt volumes from this open-hearted, self-forgetful goodness without having to put herself out in the least. "I have never been so happy in all my life!" How often did we hear those sentiments from this woman who was now in her seventies. Thus began a new chapter in her life which, in spite of her advanced years and the severe physical limitations she was under, was filled with amazing activity. To be sure, the confidence and affection shown by the Landes family towards her had a dramatic effect on Liesel. For one thing, it enabled her to rise above everything in her life to which she had so far remained unreconciled. Then again, she found true peace in accepting the way in which her life had worked out, as well as in acknowledging her temperamental weaknesses, a side of her personality which had been no easy thing for Liesel herself to bear.

In the course of time Liesel developed some skills as a counsellor, so that where someone was suffering or in need, they were able to come to her and find understanding. Indeed, even very young people who had no close relation to the Landes family came to trust in her. In this regard, I found these lines in her notebook which are relevant:

Our woe inclines to apathy;
But she has children three
Strength, patience and sympathy.

Amalie von Helwig

A further development was that her address book began to fill up quite rapidly. She never overlooked a birthday, or someone's illness, or a person who was bereaved. Yet with no false modesty she also expected the same attention from others.

There is no doubt that she sometimes demonstrated inappropriate missionary zeal. That arose on account of the fact that the many traumatic episodes in her long and hazardous life had certainly affected her perception of what faith means. Thus it was not always clear to Liesel that each person must make their own independent decision in such matters, and furthermore that a dogmatic approach to someone else's faith is unacceptable. Moreover, it is not given to everyone to have the opportunity of sharing with others from the depths of one's own experience. As it happened, those of us who were near in relation to her knew that Liesel meant well, and we rejoiced that her life was now enriched, fulfilled and provided for.

Once she wrote to my father to complain about the fact that worship in Germany since her return was meaningless to her. Here is his reply:

"... I have given a lot of thought as to why you find our Services here in Germany unhelpful. First of all, you are quite right to say that you are hearing a strange language. Remember that in Russia you had to do without speaking the German tongue for a long time. Furthermore, everything that we passed through here is quite unintelligible to you.

But there is something else. When you were in Siberia, you were able to lead an uncomplicated life that was far removed from the main events of history in the rest of the world. As far as your Christian faith was concerned, it was necessary for you to keep it strictly private. It could have no meaningful relation to the world, and was purely a matter of concern to yourself. There was no sense in which you could engage in political issues.

By contrast, in this country the purpose of the sermon is to transform the life of every one who hears it. To this end the preacher must address all sorts and conditions of people, and that means the simple as well as the educated. For example, his word should affect those who hold responsible positions in society or who have posts of leadership in business. He cannot afford to neglect the young or the old. To be precise, he is obliged to present the relevance of the Gospel to those dilemmas of existence that we are caught up in. It is in the very conflicts we are involved in with our neighbours that he must show what being a Christian means; and he must ensure that the faith of his congregation is built up as well.

In addition, a preacher is obliged to tackle the restless, questing spirit that raises so many questions in modern Western society. This is difficult, and it involves a great deal of hard work, the nature of which those who hear sermons are quite unaware of. Let there be no doubt that not every sermon will meet such exacting standards. In spite of that, if you ever get the chance to read over quietly a sermon of that nature, I believe you would change your mind ..."

I was delighted to find when I visited her one afternoon in November 1975 how contented she had become in the midst of so much that occupied her attention. She appeared to have set the past behind her as one would lay aside an old garment, and she was busy living entirely in the present. "The present moment - that is God's moment", she said.

It was when I had taken leave of her, and she had responded to my pleasure at her positive outlook on life with an appropriate comment, that she said to me with a smile that had a hint of wiliness in it: "Have I not said to you before that, as a rule, something usually happens to ensure that I do not have a smooth journey for too long?" The following day she broke her thigh.

Liesel was admitted to the hospital in Neuenstädter, and her notebook entries from the months spent there indicate how great a problem it was for her to lie flat. With her body already having suffered considerably during her time in Russia, and the small of her back causing her particular trouble, Liesel certainly had to endure a lot of pain at this time. There were occasions when she seemed to be at the end of her tether, and she shed many tears in the course of that winter spent in the hospital. Once again the old questions as to "why" all this had happened came into sharp focus. As the whole tone of her body had become weaker, she had less and less resources with which to resist her physical ailments.

Ernst and Lise Landes were daily at her bedside in spite of the severe winter temperatures which made their journey difficult. At long last spring arrived, and Liesel's condition improved. As soon as it was possible, she made contact with her fellow patients, and there were more than a few of them to whom she was able to give some counsel or comfort. Experience shows that many of these kinds of contacts made in hospital endure over the years. Doctors and nurses are not forgotten by those whom they have treated, even after they have been discharged. From now on Liesel was never without her crutch. After she had returned to Lautenbach and had settled in once again, she rarely ventured down the steep steps to the summer garden below where she used to like to sit. However, she spent correspondingly more time at her desk writing letters, for she had a real need to communicate. It should be mentioned that her statements in what she wrote at this time were more like a monologue with herself. As the thoughts of the authoress tended to wander whilst she muttered quietly to herself, she frequently lost the thread of her argument. Liesel was a diligent correspondent with people from all over the world, from Siberia to America.

In the process she never forgot to collect the far-travelled postage stamps for her nephews. She regularly sent packets to her acquaintances in Siberia, and she gave contributions to deaconess establishments as well as charities. Later when I was going through her papers the story that so often came to mind was the one that Jesus told about the widow's mite.

Liesel now began to experience increasing fatigue as the days went by. Every night it took particular patience to set her up comfortably in bed by means of pillows, cushions and blankets so that her posture was sustainable. All the same, she celebrated her 80th birthday in a manner that showed remarkable mental freshness, however frail she was becoming physically. The Landes family did so much to contribute towards what was a tasteful and congenial celebration by means of their efficient and cordial hospitality. During the evening the guest of honour related moving episodes from her life. The day closed fittingly with prayers of heartfelt thanks to God as well as an acknowledgement of the generosity of our hosts.

It was quite noticeable the way in which Liesel's strength diminished over the next months. When she broke an arm the resulting routine for those tending her was several weeks of troublesome nights. In the following year the death of her youngest brother Rudi, with whose family she formed a very close relationship, affected her deeply.

Liesel seemed to lose meaningful contact with life. She spoke few words about her death. This event appeared not to merit comment, and by all accounts she had overcome this enemy, having "passed from death to life", as John the Evangelist puts it. From this point onwards she showed an increasing patience and quietness. From time to time she still prepared small meals for herself about which she made no fuss. Obviously Liesel was no longer capable of meeting further challenges, nor were they really necessary. For in a profound sense she had "come home". "All's well that ends well", she told me one day. This remark typified Liesel and the optimism which was her hallmark.

It was a special delight for her when, on her 85th birthday in 1982, she was congratulated by name on national radio. "I never expected to be so old," she said gently. "However, please do not arrange a celebration of coffee and cakes for me today as I feel wretched." Liesel received innumerable cards and letters of congratulations, but they all remained unopened. The fact was that the old lady was now too tired to undertake anything.

Frau Landes continued to look after Liesel faithfully. Even on the evening of 6th August her valiant companion looked in unobtrusively as usual to see how she was. Her shaded night light was on, and Liesel lay awake and fully conscious. No, she did not want anything. As on many an occasion, she held in her hands at this moment a piece of paper and a pencil.

An hour later as Frau Landes again cautiously entered the room, it appeared as if the patient was fast asleep. It was only when she addressed her friend that she noticed that she was not breathing. She was shocked, for she had not anticipated that. She was quite firmly of the opinion that she would be beside Liesel when the time came for her to die. She had so wanted to be able to hold her hand and to speak comforting words to her. More than ever at the moment of her departure was it important for one who had been alone so much in life to know that she was not abandoned. And now look! She had simply made her way out of this life on her own! She had vanished as quickly as a morning vapour. This was also the anniversary day of the dropping of the bomb on Hiroshima.

Frau Landes noticed that between her hands, which were still soft, there lay a piece of paper on which was some writing. She carefully removed the paper and began to look at it. Had Liesel written a "last will"? Or were these perhaps the final sentiments of someone who, on the border of eternity, has had a special revelation? Did she have something she wanted to say, but found herself unable to express her feelings?

It was not easy to make out at first what she had written, but here are Liesel's last words, in large block capital letters:

BODY .... SOUL. ... SPIRIT: A TRINITY ...
LOVE! LOVE! LOVE!
FORGIVE ME EVERYTHING ....
I LEAVE EVER YTHI NG BEHI ND----
THER E ON HIGH - I HOP E TO SEE YOU
AL L AGA I N .....
M A Y G O D R E P A Y Y O U E V E.. R Y TH IN G ....

Liesel's final words tailed off with a random line of her pencil after "EVERYTHING" which reached right to the edge of the paper. Death's majestic stroke had lifted the pencil from her hand.

Loving hands tenderly laid her to rest in her coffin, adorning her now seemingly small form with fragrant, colourful summer flowers. Right to the very last moment of her earthly life the promise made to her had been fulfilled: "Elizabeth Thiessen, I will not leave you forlorn."

Fleetingly the thought crossed my mind as to whether there was such a thing as "vicarious suffering." I paused to consider the fact that we, her relatives, had been enjoying an endless round of happy family gatherings, delightful holidays and the many benefits of our cultural heritage, whilst for many decades Liesel had had to endure hunger, cold, poverty and desolation. To be sure, her days had ended in much happier circumstances. At the same time, when we consider such a life, with all the questions it poses, we grieve that there is no answer to the mystery surrounding it. Indeed, this side of eternity, we must accept that there will never be a full explanation.

So it was that Liesel's far-flung earthly pilgrimage -a journey that had started with all the carefree happiness of her childhood- reached its final destination in the beautiful graveyard at Bad Friedrichshall-Kochendorf, a town that still retains a rustic atmosphere. The sun shone down from a cloudless sky on a lovely summer's day as the large crowd of mourners accompanied Liesel to her grave. Such was the sense of victory that the predominant note in her funeral service was one of celebration rather than of sadness.

Nearby in the fields of Lautenbach this was the time when they were just beginning the harvest. The parallel with Liesel's story was irresistible. In that moment it was as if heaven and earth resounded with the epitaph of her life - "Those who sow in tears shall reap with joy." (Psalm 126:5)

Today pleasant summer winds and raging winter storms blow over her narrow grave. There is abundant evidence that our whole life, right to the end, consists of conflict, defeat and new beginning. Yet overall is the loving context of an unfailing promise:

"I will never fail you nor forsake you." (Hebrews 13:5)

Yesterday I visited the municipal gardens in Heilbronn once again when the flowers were in full bloom. It was here that I met my cousin Elizabeth Thiessen for the first time. This time I sat alone on the park bench.

Since then history has moved on a stage further. The accident at the nuclear power station in the Ukrainian town of Chernobyl had a devastating effect on countries in Western Europe. For one thing it confronted us with the stark reality that modern problems can only be solved together and not by mutual hostility. In addition, the vexed environmental question as to the future of this planet has come to assume ever greater importance. The urgency of this problem is grasped as much by those who live in the East as by those who are in the West. When the catastrophic earthquake shook Armenia, assistance came from every quarter of the globe. Similarly, the impending dangers of a widening ozone layer also have universal implications.

Nowadays many returning German nationals are looking for a home in a society which is already overcrowded. Will we meet the challenge of responding to their needs in an appropriate manner? Undreamed of progress has been made in the realms of technology and science. If she were alive today, Liesel's mother Anna need not have died of tuberculosis, and consequently Liesel's story would have been quite different. Instead, new and more contagious illnesses are on the horizon, and to date we are far from showing that we have the mastery of them. In and through all these spectacular advances, there is also a growing awareness that events may well have got out of control. Every day -through the very plants and creatures from which we live- we are made to feel the "groaning of creation" (Romans 8:22), a creation to which we have become debtors. Moreover, hunger and misery oppress the rapidly growing population of the world to an extent that we who live in northern Europe would rather not know about.

Is there then a solution to the threat which appears to menace us from all sides? Many a time Elizabeth Thiessen used to accuse us in the West of what she saw as a superficial existence, and of course such an irresponsible lifestyle will never provide the answers we need. To all those today who assert that "there is no one out there" who cares for us, Liesel's story is just the evidence which contradicts such a claim, and says that we need to be prepared for surprises. And her life has a further message in regard to the duty facing all of us to plan sensibly and responsibly. The fact is that the shaping of this world and its future belongs far less to us than most people would like to imagine. Therefore we simply cannot avoid taking a large step of faith, and to that end Liesel has helped me on my way.

The warmth of the sun was comforting as I sat there on the park bench. However, the light was suddenly blotted out by clouds which had swiftly moved across the sky, and soon it began to rain lightly. As I arose from my seat I was undecided as to what to do next. Should I walk on? I had actually identified this bench as the meeting-point for my family. Then out of the blue there they were. Just as my children had met me on that first encounter with Elizabeth Thiessen, so now my grandchildren came running up to me full of all the latest exciting tales and stories. We made our way together to the car.

"Look at the lovely rainbow up there in the sky!" the children called out to me. "Rainbows are formed when sun and rain come together!"

Indeed, that is exactly what happens...

"Does God keep his promises?" As she faced exile, this was the question that Liesel addressed to her elderly father.

Jacob Thiessen answered her: "You may be sure that he does."

For that reason I too will place my faith in the one who set the rainbow above our world. Yes, be it against reason to do so, and even in the face of anxiety, I will keep faith with him. Only let us keep the light of hope shining! Am I not duty bound to do this for the sake of those who have gone before me, as well as for those who come after me?

ABOUT THE AUTHOR

Charlotte Hofmann-Hege was born in 1920 to parents who were closely involved in farming and rural development in Bavaria. After a secure childhood with her brothers on an estate, Hohebuch, in Württemberg, she studied home economics and then taught for some years. In 1949 she married Helmut Hofmann, a pastor in the evangelical Lutheran church. They had three children. She died in 2012 aged 92.

Apart from the many duties of life as a pastor's wife, Charlotte devoted her writing skills to describing the impact of friends and family on her faith. She wrote 15 books, most of them having a strong biographical emphasis. By far the most popular was her narrative concerning her cousin, Elizabeth (Liesel) Thiessen, and the German edition has been through many reprints.

"The more I studied Liesel's life", Charlotte says, "the deeper the impact it made on me. I believe Liesel speaks for millions who are deprived of their rights today. Let her story give them a voice. And may it also bring courage and hope to those who are looking for a sure foundation to their lives."

ACKNOWLEDGEMENTS

I am grateful to Charlotte Hofmann-Hege for permission to translate her book, "Alles kann ein Herz ertragen", into English. I would also like to thank her daughter, Frau Martina Hofmann-Becker, for allowing me to adopt the present title of her mother's book instead of the original title. In addition, I appreciate her allowing me to include the two black and white photos of Liesel in the English edition.

It has been helpful to receive much professional assistance in producing this English edition, and I would like to express my gratitude to the following people for their contributions: Angus Ross, Fin Macrae at DUFI Art, Dangis Laurinavičius, Tom Cameron, John & Fay Henderson and Clio Gray. Every effort has been made to trace and contact copyright holders of images/photos in this publication, and I shall be glad to put right any omissions.

The author has candidly acknowledged her debt to Liesel for the wealth of enrichment she received in the course of researching her life. I would sincerely endorse that sense of indebtedness, and hope that those who read about Liesel will draw strength for their own journey.

Nick Archer
2 Aldie Cottages
Tain
IV19 1LZ

na.2ac777@btinternet.com

'We much appreciate the dedication and commitment behind the translation of this book into English. We hope that it will be read by many families in North America whose parents and grand-parents had a similar fate. It has always been my mother's wish that Liesel's life-story should inspire families to begin to search for their roots & write down their memories of those who are still alive, as a gift for the future.'

Renate Cochrane, Cape Town

153